CW00724429

THE BEST OF THE WORLD OF SHERBY57
- VOLUME 1: SHERBY GOES BANANAS.

THE BEST POSTS FROM 31ST MAY 2007
TO 30TH MAY 2009, FULLY REVISED AND
EXPANDED.

INCORPORATING

FIREHEART!

BY

STEVEN PRICE

Copyright © 2010 Steven Price. All rights reserved.
ISBN 978-1-4457-4218-2

This book could not have been completed if it wasn't for the inspiration provided by the following: Dave (Warrington legend), Si (loves pegs), Ant (for being from St Helens), Goot (evil genius), Si (lovely banana) and Nat (the gravy story)

Special thanks go to Doctor Angel for being the only person who has already read all of this rubbish and for making blogging so much fun.

Please note that this book is entirely self-edited and it's a really long, tedious process. As such, there's bound to be lots of mistakes that I missed. If you spot any, please don't be a smart-arse about it. Thanks.

Please Visit:

http://www.sherby57.co.uk

&

http://www.poursomegravyonme.co.uk

Introduction

It was way back in early June of 2007 that I first started to read *The World of Sherby57*, a blog like no other. Within just a few days, I felt that my mind and my horizons had started to widen, and my testicles started to swell in excitement. It seemed that I had finally found my spiritual home.

I have been an avid reader ever since and have marveled at its ability to be both ground-breaking and down-to earth; these two concepts had hitherto been thought to have been mutually exclusive. My mouth remains agape at its achievement.

This volume brings together some of the many highlights from *Sherby57's* first two years of existence. But it hasn't been enough for those magnificent men in their typing machines to simply reproduce what had been previously published. No, those heroic, glistening heroes that dwell within Sherby57 Towers have seen fit to re-write and extend many of the chapters that you are about to read. They do surely spoil us mortal men.

As if that wasn't enough, there is now an extended version of the thrilling *Fireheart!*, with a previously unpublished conclusion to that electrifying tale. I'm literally almost too giddy with excitement.

So, stop reading my turgid introduction and turn the page, a whole world of wonders awaits you.

Sir Rodney Cheese
Head Honcho of Cheese Industries

Computer Game Review

Computer games are big business these days, and so, not wanting to get left behind, I thought it was about time I caught up with some of the latest releases. Being an expert 'gamer', I'm in a prime position to give informed, incisive reviews. My credentials speak for themselves; I once got to level 2 on Manic Miner.

We start with *Richard Madeley's International Nose-Bleed Championship Manager 2007*, the latest release in a long line of nose-bleed simulators for the Spectrum 48K. It takes something special to make an impact in such an over-saturated market, but *Madeley 2007* has a few tricks up its sleeve. Firstly, it utilises the new Spectrum 2-D graphics card and boasts 5 separate, distinct colours; clearly making it one of the most visually stunning Spectrum titles on the market today. It is also endorsed by universally ridiculed *This Morning* presenter Richard Madeley, who adds a certain gravitas to proceedings. Anyone who is familiar with the world of professional nose-bleeding knows that Madeley is unparalleled in his knowledge of the sport. Commentary for the action sequences is provided by nose-bleed uber-fan, and *E.R.* Actor, George Clooney. This is a welcome addition to the genre for any serious nose-bleed fanatic; it has all the major European leagues available to play in and you can even participate in the EUNBA Epistaxis Championship. There is a meticulous attention to detail, from the accurate kits to the hankies used by referees; it makes you feel like you're really there. The only downside is that it may be a little too involved for the casual gamer. They should stick to *Nasal-Discharge '07*.

Sherby57 Verdict: An audacious addition to a classic genre, it really hits the spot. Should keep even the most hardened gamer happy for months – 89%

Next up is the sequel to last years surprise hit, *Office Molester*, with *Office Molester 2 – See You In Court*. The original has already gone on to be a classic, so there was an almost unbearable pressure for the developers to deliver on the sequel. Fortunately, deliver they did.

You again play as Terry Bubblenuts, a lecherous office worker who has to molest his way through twelve stories of an office block. This time, they've made the end-of-level bosses particularly tricky, with Terry having to actually get his hand into their knickers. The real improvement over the original game is the additional court room levels. Can you beat the rap? Unless you're an experienced gamer, it's unlikely. Only the very best players will be able to fondle the judge.

Sherby57 Verdict: Easily one of the best games of this or any year. You simply must add this to your collection – 95%

The final title we look at today is one of the most eagerly anticipated and overly-hyped games of all time, *Shoot My Face*. Designed specifically for the powerful Dragon 32 home computer, the aim of the game is to shoot some faces. And that's it. Each level presents you with a face which fills the screen and your job is simply to shoot it. The faces do get gradually smaller, but even by the fourth and final level, the face is still the size of a large teapot. Easy isn't the word – the word is 'too easy'. It's just not acceptable for developers to release such shoddy games in this day and age. Heads will most certainly roll.

Sherby57 Verdict: Everything about this game is a disappointment. What promised to be a frantic shoot-em-up is actually a bland, lifeless affair with poor graphics and a bad storyline. Avoid this like a bad thing - 12%

We are always being told by government busy-bodies and the nanny state that 'we', the Great British Public, should be eating so-called 'vegetables', as they are, what they call, 'healthy'. Healthy-food is a pseudo-scientific term to denote something that has been grown in the ground, and is generally made from seeds or 'plants'. Common examples that are given are sprouts, carrots, curry and potatoes. So, we all take this advice and attempt to eat 'healthily'. But, is everything really as it seems?

I recently saw some boxes that have, literally, thrown my whole world into chaos. These 'boxes' were located next to a 'spud van' - a type of street vendor who sells incinerated potatoes that, incredibly, some people eat. As I glanced over at the cardboard receptacles, I noticed a disturbing phrase embellished onto its flank. Sadly, I do not have photographic evidence of the offending statement as I was moved on (with excessive force) by the authorities. But, the three simple words are forever burned onto my memory: "The Potato Factory".

Can somebody please explain to me what a potato factory is? It makes no logical sense and it would appear that we have been lied to all along. Potatoes, if that is their real name, are supposedly grown in soil, but, in reality, they seemingly are artificially created in factories. Having only seen the side of an abandoned carton, I don't have any scientific basis for this theory, but, using common sense, I can only assume that they are cobbled together from a combination of gravel, mechanically reconstituted chicken, nuclear waste and drugs. Is this what we really want to be feeding to our children?

When I had recovered some of my composure, I decided to do some investigation. It didn't take much digging for me to come across the novel *The Potato Factory* by Bryce Courtenay. Now, I fully admit that I haven't read it, or even bothered to scan the synopsis, but, if you allow me to jump to conclusions for a moment, I think this clearly demonstrates further evidence of a worldwide potato based conspiracy.

After speaking to my network of informants, and performing some rudimentary undercover work, I was able to determine the following facts:

1. The conspiracy seems to be centered around Burscough, Lancashire.

2. People who have worked in a 'Potato Factory' all have the nick-name 'Spud', no matter how confusing it gets.

3. If asked, a 'Spud' will deny ever working in a potato factory. They will then deny being called Spud. It's like a tuber-based Fight Club.

4. A delicious variant on the potato is the 'chip'.

I must admit that I am extremely concerned about this and what it could mean for the future of democracy in this country. If I had to speculate (and I do), then I think that the 12-foot high lizards\Royal Family\NWO may be responsible. And if that lot are involved then it can only be a bad thing. Rest assured, my investigations into this scandal will continue and I have already started to assemble a crack team of anti-potato agents.

You too can play you part, and if you have any further information please get in touch.

Something traumatic happened to me yesterday.

I was mooching around the Pound Shop (as you do) and some old granny came up to me, thrusting some piece of tat into my face, and asked me: 'How much is this?'

Now, the first thought that crossed my mind (and I'm sure that it is crossing your mind as we speak) was:

IT'S A FRIGGING POUND SHOP, IT COSTS A POUND!

But then, in an instant, a second, much darker thought occurred to me. This seemingly sweet old lady actually thought I worked in a pound shop. Now, I don't want to sound insulting to anyone who actually works in a pound shop, but I'm probably going to; I was absolutely horrified that she would think such a thing.

So, after such an insult, how did I respond? Did I give her the royal ticking off that she thoroughly deserved? Did I berate her for being a decrepit, senile old witch? Did I slap her heartily across the chops and storm out of there?

No.

What I actually did was to sort of look at her funny. I'd like to think it was a look that was a mixture of disgust, horror and shame. In all honesty, I probably just looked a bit simple.

Let's just say that it wasn't my finest hour. I beat a hasty retreat.

Puzzle Corner

It's all the rage these days to do puzzle-style puzzles to improve your mental agility and erotic dexterity, and we, here at Sherby57, are not afraid to jump onto the bandwagon (as long as it isn't moving too fast). It's time to test your wits with some cunning conundrums. The answers will appear at the end of the chapter, but no cheating. Or you'll get a smack on the bum-bum.

Puzzle 1

Brian is on day-release and is very confused. Can you help him to choose the spider that leads to the red circle?

Conundrum 2

Which of the following words is the odd one out?

FROG

TURNIP

PENCIL

Riddle 3

Who am I?

Brainteaser 4

Cecil and Cecilia are looking at the ceiling. Stephen and Stephanie are walking up the steps. Harry and Harriet are being harassed. What are Joseph and Josephine doing?

Enigma 5

There are five dogs in the living room, three cats in the kitchen, four mice in the attic and a budgie in the airing cupboard. Why am I so lonely?

Make sure that you only read the answers below if you've really tried your hardest to solve the puzzles. I'll know if you haven't.

Answers:

1) The spider of choice is the one that is joining itself to the required circle of the red family. Conceptually, this would be considered the east wing of an 18th century stately home.

2) The odd word out is *hogwash* as it is the only word not visible.

3) Henry Kelly.

4) They're making sweet, sweet love.

5) It all stems back to my involvement in the Iran-Contra affair. I don't want to go into too much detail as I'm still being hounded by the press, but, suffice to say, I got my fingers burnt and I've been unable to form any human relationships ever since.

The Global Influence of Goot Crow Industries

It's one of the largest companies in the world, with a turnover of billions of dollars every year, and one of the only multi-national conglomerates to own their own planet; so, how come nobody has ever heard of Goot Crow Industries (GCI PLC)? And, more importantly, who is the shadowy figure in charge who wields so much global influence, and yet is so anonymous? He is a man that over many months of hard work we have come to know under a variety of pseudonyms such as 'Goot', 'The Crow' and 'Goot The Crow'. It hasn't been easy to get the information, but I will now attempt to unravel some of the mystery.

The Sherby57 investigative team began hearing the term 'Goot the Crow' in early 2005 through our network of sources. What was intriguing was the variety of different areas The Crow seemed to be involved in. It was our journalistic duty to dig deeper. The word was put out on the street and the team spread the globe looking for any information we could lay our hands on. Although we discovered definite links to the worlds of computing, finance and telecommunications, we were blocked at every turn when trying to find out more. Apparently the Crow was a big fish. And the kind of fish that can fly so it doesn't get caught.

Well, the Sherby57 team like a challenge and have pieced together more and more information from the scraps available. Our first aim was to locate GCI HQ. We narrowed our search to North West England but were foiled in pinpointing a location. It seems that GCI has a private wireless network which distributes its scrambled data all across the North West. We couldn't find him but at least we were making progress.

Next we tried to clarify CGI's business interests. The results were shocking. It seems that The Crow is swallowing multi-national companies in the same way that a black hole eats stars. We are not at liberty to name these companies, as we have received a legal injunction, but suffice to say that you will have eaten their food, bought their products or used their services within the last 24 hours. The phrase 'global monopoly' springs to mind.

After establishing that GCI controls such a large percentage of the world's economy, we began to wonder what sort of political influence that Goot the Crow might hold. Again we are restricted in the details that we can reveal, through not only legal pressures, but through the subtle (and no-so-subtle) death threats received daily at the Sherby57 offices. What we can say is the following:

1) Goot the Crow is the real power in North Korea.

2) The Iraq war was started to satiate CGI's oil demands.

3) Tony Blair had to resign because he wouldn't personally intervene in the 'Dell Laptop Affair'.

We dare say no more.

We urge you to help. Do you know who Goot the Crow is? Have you ever met him? Have you ever shared a Nando's with him? If so, it is your duty to tell us everything that you know. Think of the 6 billion souls on the planet who don't even know the face of their true master. It's a crime against humanity that you can help us stop.

A word of warning. If you happen to meet GTC, do not get embroiled in any of that 'cowboy shit' and think about tackling him yourself. The nefarious mogul has a constant companion: Chapatu – the catman. Chapatu is the most highly-prized bodyguard in the whole sphere of evil business. He is skilled in Kung Fu, gymnastic Boggle and erotic tennis. Suffice to say, he is considered lethal.

Stay safe out there.

Stag-Do Chic

Look out Armani, watch out Westwood: there's a new designer in town. Controversial Frenchman, Andre Ruson, has hit the streets and the kids can't get enough of his 'Stag-Do' inspired designs.

'I fink he is da best and I is likin' hiz t-shirts, man,' says Spanish teenager Losersi Moneden.

Ruson's latest collection includes the now classic 'Andy Rutter's Stag Do' t-shirt, memorably worn by MC Pork Scratchings at last year's Brit Awards. Ruson has been a big hit in the hip-hop tribute scene, with acts such as Kanye's Vest, Jay-Me and Vanilla's Nice all wearing his 'klobber'.

Originals are changing hands for as much as £500 on eBay, with rich collectors hoping to find an investment for the future. Some countries are already considering making the garments legal tender. I'm not at liberty to say which countries, but they are definitely ones that you've heard of.

This is one craze that looks like it's not going to end.

Like the BBC, Sherby57 has a remit to educate and inform, as well as entertain. Over the years, I've been asked by many people for advice on speaking the arcane language of the people of St Helens, and it's my pleasure to finally present the first in a series of lessons. I've been studying St Helensian for many years, and, even so, I don't have a full grasp of all of its nuances. There is a certain commitment needed for anyone wishing to learn even the basics, but it is certainly rewarding when you can travel over the border and communicate with the natives.

To start, I'd like to take a look at one of the fundamentals of learning any foreign tongue: ordering from the chippy. It's usually a simple task to go in to your local chip shop and ask for some food. Not so if you happen to stray into St Helens. You'd find yourself in real hot water if you're not familiar with the following two terms:

Split = Chips and Peas

Special = Potato Scallop or Fritter.

Now, they may seem straightforward, but, because they resemble words in English, confusion could ensue. For example, what would happen if you asked for a Banana Split in St Helens? Nobody wants to eat a banana with peas and chips. Not even me.

Also, be careful if you're thinking about attending the Special Olympics in St Helens. There won't be a wheelchair in sight. Instead you'll witness the local sport of racing battered potato slices around a track made from an old cardboard box.

Remember these easy rules and perhaps you'll be able to enjoy a tasty treat without humiliating yourself.

Dave Burley aka Bob aka Bobby B

Dave is one of the true stars of Sherby57 and so it's only fitting that I take time out to give a brief biography. It will certainly increase your enjoyment of some of the upcoming articles.

David Charles Burley was born in Warrington, Cheshire in 1976. Over the last 30 years he has become a local hero and a true renaissance man. His many talents have included goalkeeper, singer-songwriter, football manager, wrestling expert and radio DJ. Dave is known to some as Bob, to others as Bobby B and, to yet more, simply as Dave. He is also my friend, and makes an excellent cup of tea.

Back in the year 2000, at the height of 'Burleymania', the shops were flooded with a slew of Dave-based memorabilia. Although they haven't been officially available for several years there is a booming trade in 'Bobabelia' on eBay, with select pieces changing hands for thousands of dollars. There is a particularly rabid band of collectors in Japan, and regular conventions are held for aficionados with many enthusiasts dressing up in one of Dave's many guises.

To get a flavour of some of the items that were for sale, we now present to you a selection of the original advertisements for the Bob Products. Please be aware that there are many fakes now on the market, so please only buy from reputable dealers.

COMING SOON…

Have you always wanted to be a martial arts master? Your dream could come true, if you buy the new instructive video cassette, 'BOBIDO! – Way Of The Flying Lip.'

Learn the ancient skills of Bobido in seven easy steps. Gasp in amazement as Bob shows you how to demolish a road sign in one swift blow. Also, learn some other techniques that are, literally, too deadly to mention here.

'BOBIDO! – Way Of The Flying Lip.' - available soon from all good video outlets.

Bobstory

Face it. Your life sucks, you've got no friends and you stink. You're a loser, and there's nothing that you can do about it. Or is there?

Just when you thought that it was time to suck on a shotgun, your saviour is here. Yes, you can now listen to the glorious Dave

'Bobby B' Burley any time that you want, by making just one simple phone call. Yes, hear the man himself speak his wisdom unto you. Listen to stories that defy belief, but are actually true, on the Bobby B Hotline. For just a nominal fee ($22 per minute off-peak, $49 per minute peak) you can enjoy a transcendental experience, and maybe you'll be able to change your meaningless life for the better. Just dial…

1-800-BOBSTORY

Remember, salvation is just a phone call away.

NEW PRODUCT!!!!!

BobCorp are proud to announce an exclusive new Bobby B product. Yes, the 'BOB BURLEY NARRATES WRESTLEMANIA' Limited Edition CD box set has finally been released. This 10 CD collection contains over 12 hours of fully descriptive analysis of the wrestling world's most prestigious event. Simply perfect for any party, wedding or Bar Mitzvah.

The set comes elegantly packaged in a luxurious leatherette presentation case. Warning - this collection is limited to only 500,000 units. Order now to avoid disappointment.

Only $549.99

Although these products are long gone, please remember that Dave is available for personal appearances. Prices start from $5000 an hour, which is a bargain in anyone's book.

Television audiences may have cooled on reality TV, but the competition is certainly heating up between the two teams in the latest episode of **Celebrity Chip Shop** (Monday). With only three weeks remaining, the Red Shop and the Blue Shop are waging a bitter war to drum up custom, and while they've had limited success profits-wise, the viewer is certainly benefiting in terms of entertainment.

In a particularly amusing incident we see a scuffle break out when Keith Harris refuses to remove Orville when a customer complains about green fur in his gravy. Over in the Blue Shop, after having real problems fitting in, Ann Widdecombe finally gets into the spirit of things and creates a surprisingly smooth batter. The resulting fish are a triumph and it's hugs all around. Who will come out as the overall winner? It's too close to call at this stage, but I've got my money on Frank Bruno.

The tension was almost too much to bear when I sat down to watch the season finale of the latest hot US import **The Womb Surfer** (Tuesday). My limbs were literally melting in anticipation. If you haven't been following it, you must be brain dead, but I'll recap anyway on the off chance that you've just come out of a long term coma. It's the story of foetal detective Landau McGarnekell, who has the ability to 'surf' between the wombs of women, and uses telepathy to control them to pursue his investigations. What started as a high-concept gimmick-fest (the CGI embryo is phenomenally detailed and humourously brought to life by veteran voice-over artist Chuck Murraymint) has developed into a complex treatise on the human condition. The pressure is really on as McGarekell reaches full term, just as the serial killer 'The Nuzzler' looks to strike again. Will the 'Uteran Avenger' manage to unmask the killer before he is given birth to? I'm not going to spoil it for you, but it ends on one hell of a cliff hanger.

And so the decline of once popular soap **Peabody Place** (Monday, Tuesday – 2 episodes, Wednesday, Thursday, Friday -3 episodes, Saturday, Sunday omnibus) continues. The latest attempt to boost ratings is the Brian\Beryl\Achmed love triangle storyline that reaches its conclusion this week. Over the last few weeks, we've learned that Brian used to be a woman and Beryl announced that she is pregnant with Brian AND Achmed's babies. So boring, so predictable. Even people who don't watch the show saw *that* coming. Anyway, they've really upped the ante with Friday's episode, which ends in one of the most shocking (and gory) scenes ever seen on British television. There are apparently over 25 deaths and over 400 gallons of blood were used on set. It sounds rubbish.

Until the next time, keep watching your screens.

Welcome to lesson 2.

If your brain isn't too 'fried' from the previous lesson, I'll attempt to teach you some very basic phrases in the wonder language of the St Helener. As previously discussed, it's not an easy language to learn, so my advice is to just go with it for now. There's a good chance that it will never make sense.

Let's Begin.

Ha-woah. Wee ooo sit on da churr?

Hello. Will you sit on the chair?

Ave oo sin me diaiarry?

Have you seen my diary?

Yas iss in ma chiwowa..

Yes it's in my drawer.

Wud yu lik a mill at de Whit App ron?

Would you like a meal at the White Apron?

That's all for this time – being exposed to more than 4 phrases can literally lead to your head exploding. Read them, ingest them, love them; then come back for lesson 3.

Scientists have today announced results that prove a genetic cause for the socially embarrassing Pegwidgitis. The affliction, which compels men to clip clothes pegs on to the tips of their penises, has long been thought to have its roots in a psychological disorder. The ground breaking study conducted at Warrington's Torben Piechnik Institute has brought a glimmer of hope to those unfortunate souls that have the rare illness.

Dr Glen Medeiros, chief researcher at the institute, has been researching the problem for years after becoming acquainted, on a family holiday to Torquay, with a sufferer who reported that his son also had the same problem. We managed to interview this individual, who wishes to remain anonymous, about living with Pegwidgitis.

'I remember clearly the first time that I did it; it was the day that I first heard Milli Vanilli on the radio. I'd had the urge to do it for many years, but had resisted, thinking there was something desperately wrong with me. Anyway, this particular night, I was attending a birthday party and I'd had one too many to drink. As is usual for a birthday bash, I found myself in a shed with some friends and we were engaging in the usual shed-based tomfoolery. From the corner of my eye I could see a peg bag, teasingly hanging from a shelf. It was almost as if it was looking at me, taunting me. I could resist no longer and before I knew it a peg was hanging from my widge. It felt so damn good. It felt even better when I knew that other people were looking at my peg. Some of the others tried to make a joke of it, and I just laughed it off. But it just felt so right inside; it's just something I couldn't explain.

'After that I used to put a peg on whenever I was alone and sometimes under my clothes when I went to work. It wasn't anything sexual, it just made me feel whole. This went on for years and was my dirty little secret. Everything was fine until my wife started to notice that my foreskin had become discoloured. Apparently all that pressure had caused me to develop gangrene. I was very lucky as my GP was aware of Pegwidgitis and I was successfully diagnosed with the condition. I also got away with just being circumcised; if I had left it any longer, they would have chopped me knob off.

'My wife has always been very supportive, and, with intensive counseling, I was able to get my desires under control. It was only when we noticed that our son had the same urges that the panic set in. Was it something that I had done to him? I was worried for him but at the same time I felt very proud – it was a strange time for me. Fortunately, I met Glen on holiday, soon after. I think that because he was a stranger, and a scientist, I was able to open up to him about my woes. I was also completely shit-faced and didn't know what I was saying. It's a miracle that I was actually pouring my heart out to the one man who could make a difference, and he has been a comfort ever since. The news that he has finally made such a breakthrough is wonderful. I love him.'

A very tired Dr Medeiros said that, although they have made progress, there is still a long was to go:

'We've made progress but there is still a long way to go. Now that we have identified the genes responsible for the defect we hope to work on a cure.'

Those that suffer from this debilitating affliction will be praying for his success.

Classic Bob – The Bobby B Fan Club

We now present yet more fascinating archival material related to the height of Bobmania. This article re-prints the original advertisement for the 'Bobby B Fan Club', from way back in the year of our (imaginary) lord, 2000.

<u>The Official Bobby B Fan Club!</u>

Yes, its true! The legendary David 'Bobby B' Burley now has his own official fan-club. For a low, low one-off payment of $24.99, you will receive:

1. Membership Card.
2. Signed photo of Bob (with lipstick kiss for the ladies).
3. Free visit to the Bob Burley Museum Of Crashes.
4. Quarterly Newsletter with exclusive interviews with family, friends and the man himself.
5. Exclusive T-shirt featuring slogan 'I survived the Golf C with Bobby B'.
6. Set of 4 badges with the head of Bob.

Exciting news for all Bobby B fans! In order to thank you for being such loyal fans, Dave has composed an exclusive message, just for you:

'Thanks, to mum and dad for organising this crazy gig. RESPECT to my family, thanks to everyone for coming. And, er, enjoy the beer, enjoy the food, enjoy the do. Let's get shitfaced!

If you just had that message alone, then I'm sure that you could die happy. But, we, here at the Bobby B Fan Club, aren't content to just let you die happy. No, we want you to go in to the after-life happy, whilst thinking about Dave. To that end, we now proudly present some more exclusive content, from the man himself.

There's no way that a mere mortal could do justice to such genius, so I'll simply let Dave's poetry speak for itself. Take it away, Bob:

Get The Keys To My Jeep by Bob Burley Jr.

> Everybody put your hands up in the air
> Stevie P is the Flava of the year
> Your own personalised song lyric
> Courtesy of DJ Bobby B
> On the MIC
> In the place to be
> In the AX GT
> Friday
> I'll be looking forward to it!

I'm sure that, like me, you're literally blown away right now. While you're recovering, do yourself a favour and join the fan club. Your life will be instantly improved.

Editor's Note: I feel like I've already said this, but I'll say it again: contrary to popular belief, Dave is not an urban myth or fictional character. The message was from him, as was the poem. He really is that much of a genius.

Genetic Engineering – Has it gone too far?

It has to be said that the Sherby57 team are an open-minded, scientifically progressive bunch of guys (and gals). As an organisation, we lend our support to genetic research, and appreciate the medical benefits that it can bring to humanity.

Our world was rocked, however, when we started to receive reports about one experiment that had gone horribly wrong. Stories began to circulate about a man wandering aimlessly around the Woolston area who had a very strange appendage. Much like Big Foot, Nessie and Basil Brush, we thought that this was all an elaborate hoax. It was even postulated that the story had been dreamed up by the Woolston Tourist Board to bring visitors to the area. Completely unconvinced, we sent out an undercover investigative team in order to expose the scam. Imagine our surprise when our reporters actually gained photographic evidence of the deformed humanoid. We dare not re-print the photo here, it could mentally scar those of a nervous disposition.

When the photograph was sent back to Sherby57 HQ, we were genuinely shocked and horrified. Much like dropping shampoo into the eyes of rats, can anyone see a valid reason for giving a human man a banana penis?

Mr Banana-Penis, as he came to be known, was pictured with an inane grin on his poor, deluded face. Did he even realise the nature of the crimes that had been perpetrated against him? It seems unlikely; he looked too stupid.

The most obvious question was staring at us uncomfortably in the face: would a banana penis even be functional? And, if it was, what would the offspring of such a fruity phallus look like? It's only in the realm of the madman to speculate.

After overcoming our natural revulsion to this crime against nature, we had no other choice than to help Mr B-P. We immediately contacted our good friend, Dr Glen Madeiros, who mobilised his best men to work on the problem. How could such a creature be captured? The answer was remarkably simple. A team of highly-evolved chimps (courtesy of the Torben Piechnik Institute) were dispatched to the area. Each chimp was tagged with a GPS homing beacon that could be used to track each individual's movements.

Now comes the science bit. Dr Madeiros had created a sophisticated computer program that could interpolate from the chimps' movements the location of Mr B-P. The theory was that each chimp was spread out throughout the Woolston region and they would naturally be drawn to the freshest banana in the area. Once they had a sniff of Mr B-P, it was simply a race against time to reach him before the chimps did and thus preventing an unpleasant scene.

Luckily, the chimp handlers reached Mr B-P with just seconds to spare and he was quickly placated with a bag of Haribos.

We are assured that the young man in question has been re-homed in a donkey sanctuary in Devon, far away from the prying eyes of the media, and that he is recovering well.

Let this tragedy be a warning to all of us.

Editor's Note: Since this story was originally published online, it has received 3167 hits (at the time of writing). Since many of this hits were from people searching for masturbatory aids, I cannot help but think that the story was actually rather exploitative of poor old Mr B-P.

Thumping Hearts – An Exclusive Extract

Sherby57 are proud to present an exclusive extract from Thumping Hearts, the new novel from romance supremo Eve St. Prince.

Brian stood on the balcony. He was as naked as the day he was born - except for his trademark Trilby. He let out a deliciously satisfied sigh and lit his pipe, drawing deep on the aromatic cherry-flavoured smoke.

'Mmmm. One Stop News sell the finest tobacco,' he said to himself. He blew the smoke from his full, sensuous lips into a massive cloud, pungent with his over-ripe sexuality, and looked out over the Monte Carlo coastline. It was a simply exquisite view, but then you'd expect nothing less from the balcony of the most expensive suite in the exclusive Hotel Du Le Conga. The suite was costing him literally an arm and a leg, but Sandra was worth it. Sandra was worth anything.

His heart pounded rhythmically whenever he thought of her and his battle-scarred member grew proud. He felt sightly self-conscious of his manhood and had done ever since that fateful day in Normandy. He knew it didn't matter to Sandra, though, and the thought of her devotion only made him harder. He could feel the lining of his Trilby becoming swamped in erotic sweat as her face swam in his imagination.

As if telepathically connected, Sandra joined him on the balcony wearing naught but a bathrobe, her mousy hair glistening in the moonlight.

'I wouldn't go in the bathroom for ten minutes,' she whispered, blushing. 'I nearly blocked the drain.'

'Oh darling,' exclaimed Brian, pulling her close to him and his rigid love rod. 'You're so silly. Lets go inside.'

The room was immaculate. The walls, floors and bed were all made of luxurious Italian marble. Even the marbles were made of marble and Brian looked forward to a game after they had made sweet love. He hoped to win back his best steely that he had lost to the porter, the night before.

Brian lifted Sandra and placed her gently on the bed. 'Jesus, she's put on a bit of tonnage,' he thought to himself with a smile. She was still the most beautiful animal he had ever seen and that included a race horse, so he thought she was pretty special. She looked up at him and smiled, breathlessly.

'Take me, Brian. Take me,' she said, her breasts flapping gently in the wind.

'Where to? I thought that we were going to stay here and, you know, do it,' he replied. He immediately realised his mistake and they both laughed.

Taking the initiative, Sandra slowly unwrapped her robe and lay ready for entry. Brian held her closely and she gasped as she felt his throbbing utensil.

Their love spilled over.

Thumping Hearts is released next week by Sherby57 Books.

Bullseye Bollocks

It seems to be all the rage these days to go on about Bullseye and how great\funny it was. When people discuss it they tend to make comments along the lines of:

'BFH! Ha ha, bus fare home. What's all that about?'

'And then... and then... they won a speedboat!! They live in Birmingham. Ha ha.'

'Super smashing great! Ha ha.'

'Lets have a look at what you could of won! Ha ha.'

'Iiiiiiiiiiiin one... a shit prize.. ha ha.'

Etc.

Brilliant.

Can I just go on record to say that Bullseye was (and is) one of the worst television programmes ever and it was the bane of my childhood Sunday afternoons. Back in those days we only had one television and for some reason my dad insisted on watching it every week.

Of course I could have gone and read a book or played out, instead of watching telly, but, get real, that wasn't going to happen.

It's not big or clever to act as if watching Bullseye was a cherished memory from your youth. It wasn't. It was crap.

Thanks for listening.

Pop Shop Plop – A Poem

I want to drink some pop

So, I'll get some from the shop

But first I need a plop

When will I stop?

I need to get a job

But I am a fucking knob

So I ate a corned beef cob

Which made me start to sob

My mate's name is Stan

He cooks with a pan

He also is a man

And he has a lovely tan

My wife's name is Pam

She really stinks of Spam

Yet, she only eats ham

And I cover her in Jam

Now I've drank some pop

I got it from the shop

I also had a plop

Now it's time to stop

One Was A Stunner, One Was a Dog – A Brainteaser

A man walks into a pub, accompanied by several of his work colleagues. The group enjoy an wonderful evening of drinking and dancing in the said public house. The man does not leave the sight of his colleagues for more than 2-3 minutes in the whole night (allowing for toilet breaks). They all leave at the end of the evening, a little worse for wear.

On the following Monday morning, the man tells his workmates that he had sexual relations with two women within the pub, on that very same night out. The only clue that he leaves is the enigmatic statement: 'One was a stunner, one was a dog.'

How could this possibly have happened?

Editor's Note: This puzzle was finally solved by Dr Angel on the 14th August 2009, almost two years after it was first published. If you'd like to know the answer, go to www.sherby57.co.uk and search for 'Stunner Dog'.

Join ESA – Earth Song Anonymous

Are you prone to any of the following?

1. Dropping to your knees and wailing whenever you see an elephant on television.
2. Using the phrase 'What have we done to the world?' in inappropriate conversations.
3. Walking around devastated rain forests in white shirts.
4. Singing 'ooooooooooooooo… ooooooooooooooo' when you are supposed to be working.

If you answered yes to one or more of them, you may be addicted to Earth Song. This is an increasingly common affliction and it is high-time it was seriously addressed.

Now, at this stage, a large proportion of people would react by saying: 'Yes, I have the symptoms, but I don't even like Earth Song!' And, in a logical world, this would be a valid argument. Sadly, we don't live in a logical world, and the very fact that you don't like it actually makes it more likely that you are an addict. Please, do not panic. Help is at hand.

At ESA, we truly understand how you feel. Every single one of our fully trained counsellors is a recovering Earth Song addict. It's a disease that can't be cured but you can learn to live with it. With our patented 13 step program, you can regain control of your life and your families will start to love you again. Probably.

Join today. We're here to help.

Goot Crow Oz

G'day

This is an official warning to all Australian cobbers of Sherby57. The sinister business magnate\tribal warlord Goot 'Goot The Crow' Crow is on his way to your lovely country. We advise extreme caution for the next few weeks as we have not been able to fully account for his whereabouts.

Thousands of rumours have flooded the internet and we have been carefully sifting through them to separate the wheat from the chaff. One of the most persistent stories is that he intends to purchase Uluru, aka Ayers Rock, and rename it 'Goots Rock' or 'Gooturu'. Some conspiracy theorists claim that the reason he wants to buy the rock formation is to hollow it out and create an underground HQ, in which he could survive a nuclear holocaust. Others suggestions add that he is going to trigger the atomic apocalypse himself.

Yet more gossip has linked Goot to Aussie fashion designer Joshua Goot . Are they related? We have no evidence of it, but it seems too incredible to be a coincidence. Either way, it's an intriguing new development.

Our antipodean correspondents are now on red alert. We are determined to get to the bottom of his nefarious plans, and to stop him, if we can. Stay tuned and stay safe. We must protect Toby Mangel, at all costs.

On you wild man!

Editor's Note: This was originally published in October 2007. As of writing, Australia is still an independent nation and there has been no nuclear winter. Toby Mangel remains at large.

The Sea... see? - A Poem

The Sea... the Sea

Cold black tendrils eating my heart

The Sea ... the Sea?

It don't matter to me – he

Invalid Addresses, multiplying exponentially

Where is my father?

Yes, yes, the dripping blackness enters my soul

The sea. See?

No

I do not

What on earth are you on about?

How Posh?

As I go about my daily life, I often get stopped in the street and mistaken for royalty. It really is a most awful burden; my natural regal elegance and haughty speaking voice often rubs the proles up the wrong way. And you wouldn't even want to rub them up the right way.

Others choose to attack me and squawk: 'How posh are you really? You're just a big stink nose!' Once and for all, I intend to answer these critics.

My answer to these cretins is this: a close personal friend of moi actually lives on the same estate where puppeteer extraordinaire Bob Carolgees used to live.

Take a moment to think about it and let the facts soak in. Are you ready to continue? OK.

Now, I ask you, given the information which I have just imparted to you, is it possible for me to be any more of an aristocrat?

I think not.

Now toddle off, you oiks, and get back down t'pit.

Yours

Sir Smedley-Sherby57

Today's lesson features a commonly used phrase by the St Helener that is utterly baffling to the outsider. Yes, today we address the infamous 'Fe Te' – the unnecessary addition.

So, you've learned a reasonable vocabulary and have a decent grasp of the grammatical basics. In a fit a unwarranted confidence, you decide to approach the nearest person from St Helens and attempt to converse with them. All is going well and you're feeling awfully smug about your own abilities as a linguist. Then it happens. Out of nowhere, you hear them slip the words 'Fe Te' into a sentence and your whole world falls apart. As you lie on the floor, tears streaming down your face, you'll wish that you read this lesson before you got so bloody cocky.

To help explain 'Fe Te', I'll use an example:

'Am gowan the shop to fe te get sum milk.'

In English this means:

'I'm going to the shop to get some milk.'

As you can hopefully see, the 'Fe Te' is essentially just there to fill space. All you need to remember, for a successful conversation, is that these extra words are completely unwarranted and you can carry on your conversation as if they didn't exist.

Be warned, there are no rules to follow when using the 'Fe Te' – it's almost something that is genetically built it to the St Helener. Please do not be tempted to use it yourself – you will definitely make a fool of yourself and you could be banished from St Helens forever. None of us would want for that to happen.

Good Luck!

When we last left **The Womb Surfer** (Tuesday) it was the thrilling first season finale. The foetal detective managed to apprehend the mysterious serial killer 'The Nuzzler', who, in a brilliant twist, turned out to be Florence McGarnekell - Chief of Police - and his mother! Well, Season 2 has just gotten underway and I thought I'd check it out to see if it could pick up right where it left off. I wish I hadn't bothered; it was the biggest disappointment since that fortnight I had in Greece a few years ago. It's a tragedy to see a once great format utterly ruined. The second season makes 'Look Who's Talking' look like 'The Godfather'.

The cliffhanger from season one, in which Landau was born in prison, was too quickly brushed aside and it left me with a bitter taste in my mouth (not literally). When will the network executives learn that they don't need to meddle with great art for the sake of ratings?

The action has unceremoniously been moved forward by several months and we are, somewhat implausibly, asked to believe that a baby could open a detective agency in downtown LA. The shift to the agency comes with a completely new supporting cast. Firstly, there is the secretary, Bamby, who may be a great piece of eye candy but even the most red-blooded of males will be bemused as to why she goes to the office wearing only scant items of lingerie. Next is 'Crusty Joe', the building's janitor and supposed comic relief. I've had hemorrhoids that were funnier. Last, and by no means least, there is 'John O'Groats', Landau's new partner and who just happens to be a dog! In a tedious twist, the dog is the only character who can communicate with the pre-speech McGarnekell. You could possibly suspend disbelief, but the stupidity is compounded when you realise that because McGarnekell also can't speak, neither of the two principal characters has any lines. It certainly doesn't make for a very interesting show when your two lead characters can't actually speak. To say that they haven't thought it through is something of an understatement. I'm starting to think that this is one show that should have been aborted.

On a lighter note, new hidden camera show **You Wish You Were Dead** (Saturday) takes the seemingly moribund genre to dizzying new heights (or should that be sickeningly low lows?). It's surprisingly bold for prime time Saturday viewing; one skit features a man reduced to tears as he is stripped naked, then bound and gagged, before passers-by are invited to catapult human faeces at him. The man pleads and begs for his torment to stop as his family encourage people to 'go for the eyes'. It's hilarious stuff.

Finally, for this week, we take a look at the harrowing documentary **Men and Their Mugs** (Sunday). It's a little known fact that as many as one-in-four of the adult male population have love affairs with their favourite mugs. We meet Terry, who's had a steady relationship with a blue Chester Zoo mug called Sandra for 14 years. He claims that they're happy together, even though they can't have children. Terry would like to adopt but Sandra isn't so sure. It's a fascinating insight in to a previously hidden world.

Until next time, keep your eyes square and your fingers squarer.

What happened was this, right. There I was, just minding my own business, when I heard this, like, siren thing going off, and I said, 'I bet that's a fire alarm.'

My mate looks at me, then looks around, then back at me. He's puzzled 'cos he can't like see no buildings or nothing. So, he says to me, 'Whose fire alarm?', 'cos, like, he can't see who on earth would have a fire alarm.

But then, and this is the key part, then me other mate thinks he has said, 'Who's Faria Alam?' and so he says 'She shagged the FA!'

And so, really, it was just all one big misunderstanding.

Pour Some Gravy On Me

You may remember, a few weeks ago, that I was informing all you peasants just how upper class I am (go back and read *How Posh?* - you probably don't remember). Well, you lucky people, here is further evidence, not that you need it. What what.

A few days ago, one was dining in an exclusive restaurant (I can't name it, it's far too exclusive for the likes of you to even know about) and the waiter asked me, 'Would you like gravy with that, Sir?'

'Gravy?' I said. 'GRAVY?? I don't even know what this *gravy* is, you absolute clot.'

And I don't know what it is. For all I know, it could be a kind of bread roll, a type of potato or even a sauce.

Do you have any idea of how posh you have to be not to know what gravy is? I'm virtually fucking royalty, pal.

Editor's Note: This post proved to be the inspiration for the excellent blog, Pour Some Gravy On Me. You should visit it at http://www.poursomegravyonme.co.uk.

I plunge my lust into the ring pull

The aluminium sheath buckles and opens for my thirst

Wide, very wide

I hear the fizz, the fizz it beckons me

The sounds of war, the pain of peace.

The tang of metal on my succulent lips

Why does this yearning consume my soul?

The sticky, sweet liquid satiates my desire

Liquid becomes solid, solid becomes anger

I rest, a lion that has devoured its prey

Forgive me my love, forgive me

The cycle must begin again

Hallo!

I am enthusiastically welcoming all my good Englisher chums and thanking them for reading. This is Tuesday und mein name must be Hans Klaussner. Ja, das ist korrekt; I am being from Germany. Ha ha ha ha ha ha, you English with your senses of humours. You are most certainly making me wet with pleasure in the groinal zone.

Ladies from England: beware! Hans is being on the loose and he is looking for love. From you. I must insist that you enter my domain where we have much happiness and wiener schnitzel together for eternity. Hahahahaha ha ha ha. I think so.

Please be do not think I am like big fat man shitting in a top hat. I am good man and I like to treat the fraulein in the correct manner in accordance with the sacred Bavarian tradition.

Hans has the biggest intention to move to the England when is possible and he is am wanting to meet wife for love and marriage. Like a horse and the carriage, as your prime minister, Al Bundy, is saying. Haha ha ha ha. I am making the joke.

But not about love. Love is a battlefield and I will fight with the German people in my heart for you is being my love.

If you please, is reply to Hans and is talk to me for date?

Yours lovingly,

Hans Klaussner.

Ramsay's Not So Posh

Something curious happened last night. I had just finished watching a nature documentary and was waiting for a programme about the Royal Family to start. In order to kill a few dastardly seconds, I happened to flick on to something called 'Channel 4' and found an awful show called 'Ramsay's Kitchen Nightmares'. This chap, who is known as Gordon Ramsay, goes to some unsavoury (pun intended) restaurant and attempts to turn around their fortunes. In this particular episode Mr Ramsay suggested that the restauranteur (it was actually a public house – how gauche!) started a 'Campaign for Real Gravy'.

Now, as you know, I have no concept on what this 'gravy' is (see *Pour Some Gravy On Me*), but, regardless of what it is, I consider it to be beneath someone of my social standing.

What really irks me is that after some research I've discovered that this oik Ramsay actually has a restaurant with 3 Michelin stars. Now, I wouldn't eat anywhere that has less than 4 Michelin stars, but even so I find this shocking. How can they give these awards to someone who promotes 'gravy'? I will be writing to my good friend Henry Michelin forthwith to demand that Gordon and his cronies are stripped of their stars. If my demands are refused then I will certainly make sure I that I buy Pirelli tyres from then on.

Fight this monstrosity of a man, for all that is good and holy.

There's something of a change of pace for today's lesson, as we take a look at the bizarre world of St Helensian cuisine. In particular, we're going to examine their traditional, national dish, Cremated Breast of Lamb.

Breast of Lamb is an unpopular cut of meat in most sane cultures. In fact, calling it 'meat' at all is stretching the truth to breaking point and beyond. In case you've never actually encountered the BoL before, it is essentially a roll of lamb fat with a scraping of meat on the inside. It has been described by culinary experts as, 'A strange joint which is pretty nearly inedible.' There are a few recipes that exist for the BoL in the wider world, but these generally involve slow cooking the meat and serving as a roast with vegetables. This is not the St Helens way.

The St. Helener has a particular love of eating fat, indeed they often throw the meat away and just eat the fat. Anthropologists believe that these strange eating habits may have first been acquired as a method of stocking up on fuel prior to the traditional winter hibernation.

The traditional Breast Of Lamb recipe involves putting it in to an oven on high heat and cooking the joint until it is rock hard (apparently this diamond hard crust is the best part). Once this is complete it is 'plonked' onto a plate with no trimmings or side dishes and is immediately devoured.

I'd suggest that you try it for yourself, but that would just be stupid.

Mike Robot

Dear Nile,

My name is Mike Robot. I am called Mike and I am a robot. I want to be your special friend. I promise that I will be a good boy-robot.

Mike Robot works very hard for you. My programming make me love you, like a puppy loves his master. But, I no do no damage to your furniture.

It was not me, Nile. I promise.

I did not break it.

I am programmed to make phone calls, many times. But they are nice and I like them and speaking to real human people. I am good Mike Robot. Do not be nasty. Please give me job in your factory, Nile. I am very strong.

I love you,

Mike Robot.

That was a party political broadcast on behalf of Mike Robot (The Boy Robot).

Ever since I published the story *'Genetic Engineering – Has It Gone too Far?'* I've been inundated with letters, e-mails and faxes, all demanding an update on the fate of poor old Mr Banana-Penis.

There's also been a surge of interest in the article via internet searches. Over the last few days, the popularity of this story has soared. People have been searching from as far afield as Poland, Australia and Japan. Mr B-P is turning into a truly global phenomenon. Admittedly, some of those hits are from perverts who just want to see a banana-like penis, but I'm really not responsible for that sort of thing.

Anyway, with such an overwhelming demand for information, it would be remiss of me not to provide an update. I've been in touch with Mr B-P, who has moved from his donkey sanctuary in Devon to the world-renowned Torben Piechnik Institute under the care of Dr. Glen Medeiros. After leading a somewhat tragic life, Mr B-P is literally cock-a-hoop at all the attention that his penis is receiving and is ecstatic that so many ladies from around the world are gazing upon him with such admiration. I didn't have the heart to tell him that the chances are that it would mainly be men who were looking at him. That would just be cruel.

Unsurprisingly, Mr B-P is currently single and has asked me to put out a request to all his female cock-gazers to get in touch. He'd love to meet you and to possibly show you his yellow glory. At present he would like to keep his true name secret, so any correspondence will have to be initiated through this book's author.

In attempt to drum up some more lady-interest for him, I will now tantalize you with some more details. He is said to closely resemble Spanish teen fashion expert, Losersi Moneden. He is 28-years old, has his own teeth and can read (to a very basic level). He has his own, semi-furnished room at the Institute (based in Warrington, England) and is allowed to go out on dates pretty much when he wants. He does have to let the doctors know in advance if he is planned on taking someone back to his room. It's essential that any B-P action is recorded for posterity to see how it 'stands up' to the task. If this makes you a little uncertain, I have been assured by the Institute that the B-P is fully functional and 'has a good length and girth', but with the bonus of a 0% chance of pregnancy or STDs (banana seeds are totally safe to humans).

Please get in touch if you think you'd like to meet him. He's a really nice fella, and is surprisingly well adjusted given the circumstances. There's no pressure but he's looking to settle down and meet Miss Right. And when I say 'Miss Right', I mean someone who is a Miss and is right for him. He's not specifically looking for somebody called Miss Right. That would be ludicrous.

Anyway, fingers crossed that Mr B-P finds his true love and that I'll soon be buying a new hat for the first Sherby57 wedding.

The Sherbys 2007

The Date: 27th December 2007

The Place: London's magnificent O2 Arena

The Occasion: The 72nd Annual Sherby57 Awards 2007 aka The Sherbys

Yes, in a star-studded ceremony hosted by Sir Trevor McDonald and Jodie Marsh, the year's most prestigious awards were presented in front of a 23,000 capacity crowd and the world's press. Unfortunately due to phone poll rigging allegations in previous year's awards, the event was not televised. Instead, I provide edited highlights of the winners and losers of the awards that it is sensible to comment on in a book that doesn't have any pictures.

TV Show of the Year

It has been a troubled year for the world of broadcasting: the Big Brother race row, Blue Peter's faked competition and a hardcore anal sex scene on Emmerdale. Despite all the controversy, there have been a few genuine nuggets of televisual gold. And here they are:

Runners-Up:

Celebrity Chip Shop – A triumphant return for the celebrity reality show, this show blew the others away, both in terms of ratings and intrigue. The competition was neck and neck right to the closing moments of the final episode, when the Red Team just about scraped a victory by a ball-clenchingly slim margin of just 12 pence.

You Wish You Were Dead – With viewing figures of over 20 million, this comedy juggernaut harked back to a golden era of television. However, the content of the show would not have gone down well in our more genteel past as it provided ratings and cruelty in equal measure. Indeed, one, now infamous, episode provided us with the 'water-cooler moment' of the year, with a prank that involved faking a fatal car crash and convincing a man that his entire family were dead. Utterly hilarious, but it wasn't quite able to take the award.

And the Winner is:

The Womb Surfer – the outstanding drama of the year, this US import has received both critical and popular acclaim. Despite a somewhat ridiculous start to the second season, the show has continued to wow audiences and is a worthy winner of this award. So, it was no surprise when the crowd at the O2 arena went wild when its stars, Chuck Murraymint and Danny Spencer, appeared in person to collect their trophy. The actors, who play Landau McGarnekell and John O'Groats respectively, had to wait for a full 73 minutes for their standing ovation to subside, before being able give their acceptance speech. Murraymint said 'Thanks', while Spencer said 'Woof woof.'

<u>Comment of the Year</u>

When many of these articles originally appeared in blog-form, there was opportunity for Sherby57's myriad of fans to leave a comment on them. As we pride ourselves on being a democratic organisation, it seems only fitting that the best of those comments receive the recognition that they deserve.

Runners-Up:

A Local Tramp commented on 'One was a Stunner, One was a Dog – A Brainteaser':

Hi there Sherbs! Just spotted this discussion and I think I may have something to add. I remember one night a good few years ago when I was in bed just by the bins at the back of the Postern Gate Pub in Warrington. I was woke up by what appeared to be a balding man, a stunner and a dog! The man kept saying things that I couldn't quite make out – I'm sure I did catch a few phrases though such as: 'Four Letters …. Loser', 'Alright stunner – Have a nice weekend?', 'Alright dog – Have a nice weekend?' and 'Me and me mate went Jet-Skiing this weekend'. Didn't see any activities of a sexual nature though! Hope this helps!"

The Speak Man commented on 'Where Do Spuds Come From?':

Mr Sherby – obviously your investigatory skills are amazing. Please please please could you finally investigate and give an answer to the following question that has haunted my night times for the past three years – "why were Phil and Tony left out of the loop??" I think we all need to know and so we can all finally lay this one to rest!!

And the Winner is:

Dionne Warwick on 'Bullseye Bollocks':

You forgot to say 'stay out on the black and into the red, nothing in this game for two in a bed'. I concur that Bullseye is poo with a very low production value to match the IQ of the contestants. However I would have liked to know how the contestants shared the prize of a caravan. May I suggest a time share arrangement? this would mean that all parties could spend quality time in the luxurious two bed caravan located at Robin Hood caravan park, Prestatyn. here they could also make good use of the 1.5 person speedboat, max speed 10 MPH with white leather seat with built in lager can holder and chipstick dispenser. A tub of vaseline is also advisable, to apply after you have eaten the chipsticks.

I would like to know your thoughts on another show now deemed to grace the halls of cooldom, blockbusters with bob holness, can I have a P please bob, can I have a E please bob, you get the picture!!!

In a hard fought category there were many worthy winners. Ultimately, though, I hate Bullseye and there can only be one winner. Unfortunately the holidays are Miss Warwick's special time and she spends the festivities at home with her family, so wasn't able to attend the ceremony. However she did send her thanks.

News Story of the Year

There have been some huge stories in the news this year; Gordon Brown becoming PM, the floods, the missing rice scandal etc etc. As always, though, the Sherby57 investigative team were at the forefront of quality journalism. This award is a tribute to those precious stories that made a difference in your pathetic lives.

Runners-Up:

Where Do Spuds Come From? – A dazzling expose on the whole corrupt potato industry. Eating a chip will never be the same again. Although they will still taste as great.

Peggy Widge – An insight into a rare and disturbing medical condition. Thought provoking, but slightly perverted.

And the Winner is:

The Global Influence of Goot Crow Industries – This is the groundbreaking report that first informed the world that their lives are not their own. The Crow is a tough (metaphorical) nut to crack and he has been soaking in (actual) vinegar. The Sherby statuette was collected by the whole Sherby57 team as the crowd chanted 'thank you'. They can save the world with your help.

<u>Villain of the Year</u>

Boooooooooooo.

Hisss.

Runners-Up:

Mike Robot – He claims that he is innocent and is a 'good boy -robot', but does anybody believe him? Sinister squared.

Mr Quiff – He's yellow. He has a quiff. He is very rude. He makes my skin crawl. He's so evil that this is the only mention of him that you'll find in the entire book.

And the Winner is:

Goot the Crow – Well, this wasn't really in any doubt, was it? He has his fingers in more pies than Jack Horner (who admittedly was only using his thumb). And they all stink. His fingers stink, not the pies. Anyway, think of a combination of Hitler, Stalin, Mao and Keith Chegwin. Multiply by a million. Cover it in Satan Shit and mix it all together. Dress it up in an SS uniform with a Gary Glitter wig. And Goot would still call it a cissy.

It goes without saying that he didn't collect the award in person.

<u>Hero of the Year</u>

It's the final and most prestigious Sherby of all. The tension is almost unbearable, so I'll just get on with it.

Runners-Up:

Hans Klaussner – This plucky German warmed all out hearts as he unsuccessfully looked for love. Bravery in face of adversity and a way with words has made Hans a national treasure in a nation that is not his own.

Dr Glen Medeiros – Finally, a scientist that truly understands the vagaries of the human heart. It's truly breathtaking how one man can so successfully combine infinite compassion with the cold hard logic of an absolute bastard. His varied humanitarian work ranged from those who put pegs on their penises to those who have a banana for a penis. It has to be said that it's generally penis-based. His work at the world-renowned Torben Piechnik Institute is an inspiration to us all.

And the Winner is:

Dave "Dave" Burley – Dave is the worthiest of winners. What more can I write about him that I haven't already written endlessly about. I don't think that messiah would be too strong a word. Dave graciously appeared in person at the ceremony and received an unprecedented four hour standing ovation. Many of those in attendance patiently queued up to wash his feet or to be healed. He sang, he laughed, he cried. He touched us all. Not literally, I mean emotionally. He's not a sex pest.

Eventually the crowd eventually settled down, and a hush descended over the arena as everybody realised that Dave was about to impart a message. It was a simple message but one that will echo down through the ages:

'Enjoy the drink. Enjoy the dancing. Enjoy the do. Let's get shitfaced.'

And on that emotional note the ceremony was drawn to a close and the red carpet was rolled up until next year.

All the best. Have a good one. Take care. And, if I don't see you, happy New Year!

Obviously, I'm only saying all this just to be polite. What exactly is the deal with 'New Year'? Has anyone, other than me, actually stopped and asked themselves what they actually think they are celebrating? If I was of a more conspiratorial bent, I'm sure I'd suspect that the 12-foot lizards were behind all this unwarranted revelry. Vast swathes of the populace celebrate the ticking over of another year (a totally arbitrary measurement) with the glazed-eye zeal of a fundamentalist christian.

New Year is not the only 'event' that people celebrate blindly because they are told to. The new pagan-cult holidays also consist of Valentine's Day, Mother's Day and Halloween. The amount of time and effort (and money) put in to celebrating these non-entities is nothing short of disgusting. Do I really need to prove that I love my mum by mindlessly following the herd and buying flowers on mothers day? Does buying roses and going for a meal like every other idiot in the country really prove devotion to a loved one? I really don't think so.

And yes, I am in a mood because I am back in work.

All the best!

Hans Klaussner – Han That Does Dishes

Hallo and willkommen to all my new chums.

Ich bin Hans Klaussner und I am still looking for the love. Ha ha ha. That is correct.

Since we have last have been speaking, Hans has made great leap across pond and is now residing in the Land of Eng (England, my friends ha ha). I am working as a waitress in a cocktail bar, that much is true. Ha ha, this much is certainly not being true. I am making big German joke that I am hoping that you are liking. For reality's sake, I am working in a restaurant kitchen where I am currently the head of the section that is washing the pots and pans.

I am making many new friends in my working place. My good friend is the chef, known by his name of Cheface. He is also like me, not from being born in UK. Alas! He does not speak with any known language and so I am still unknowing of his origin of country. Cheface is not shouting and using badwords like the man Ram-Say. Yes? Although this is not being so certain since he is not speaking any words that we are all knowing! Hahahahahaha. Crazy.

Information: I am still looking for love with a delicious rose of England. Is you please e-mail Hans if you is also lonely lady? I am good man and will provide many furs and warmth for the winter festival.

Speaking to you soon.

Hans

P.S.

When in my restaurant, please do not ask for any dish containing squid. Is very big problem. Danke.

Sherby57 Day Trip – Kayak The Amazon

Dear All

I have been looking in to booking a day trip some time in July to go kayaking in the Amazon. I have been in contact with experienced adventure holiday company 'Deliverance Tours' and I've been able to negotiate a really great price as July is monsoon season.

The itinerary is as follows:

Arrive in Bogotá at 8am and are driven via mini-bus to the river. There will be opportunity to sample the local "marching powder".

8:30-12:30 – Canoe through Columbia, Ecuador, Peru and Bolivia at a leisurely pace.

12:30-13:30 – A one hour stop-off on the river bank for a picnic lunch (included) and sight-seeing. The inclusive lunch consists of: 1 Ham Sandwich, 1 Cheese Sandwich, 1 Apple, 1 Mars Bar (or local equivalent), 1 Gutalamalan Insanity Pepper

13:30-17:30 – Continue to explore the rich flora and fauna of the Amazon Rain Forest whilst canoeing down river. Don't miss your chance to lick a tree frog (if time permits).

17:30 – Arrive at Rio de Janeiro for complimentary BBQ in front of that massive statue of Jesus. The flight home is approx 20:30 (which means that we should be home in time for the ten o'clock news).

The cost of the trip should be around £4000, so please let me know asap if you are interested so I can firm up the details.

Whoops Julius!

I've had this song going around in my head for days, but nobody else seems to know it. It's so frustrating. Surely there is somebody who remembers this old tune:

When you're feeling kind of peckish

And you don't know what to eat

There's only one thing that you can get

That's going to give you a treat

Oh, a Julius for lunch

A Julius for lunch

A salad you'll remember!

Just make sure you hold the cucumber

Julius for lunch.

Erm... Just me then?

People often like to play the game 'What if?' What if the Nazis had won the second world war? What if JFK hadn't been assassinated? What if *Groove Is In The Heart* had been judged number one instead of *The Joker*? I guess we'll never know.

One of the things that I've always wondered is what the world would be like if the USA had been founded by Roy Walker? I think it would have probably been something like this:

(to the tune of the Star Spangled Banner)

Oh, say what you see

What is Mr Chips doing?

Riiiiiiiiiii-ight!

Let's have a-nother catchphrase.

I think we can all agree that the world would be a much safer and happier place. If only somebody could invent some kind of crazy time machine. I'd quite happily volunteer to go and tinker with the space-time continuum.

In the latest of our medical updates from the hard working staff at the Torben Piechnik Institute we tell the upsetting story of Blind-Duh-Date Syndrome. This is a recently discovered mental condition in which sufferers talk in a strange speech pattern totally out of their control. Lead researcher, Dr Shirley Pepsi, explains:

'The condition usually affects people in their early 20s, generally those who have no history of mental health issues, who find themselves suddenly unable to communicate without asking a question in the style of a Blind Date contestant. It sounds amusing to begin with but it rapidly causes personal problems and breakdowns in formerly stable relationships.'

Dr Pepsi was kind enough to show us around the Grotbags Ward at the Institute which specializes in treating BDD sufferers. We spoke to a Mr Smith Jooooooones, a former football scout, and asked in which ways the the condition affected him:

'I'm unable to have a normal conversation. If you were unable to have a normal conversation, what type of unusual conversation would you have and why? That goes to number one.'

There is no drug available to treat the disorder and Dr Pepsi is using an unusual therapy technique where the patient talks to three clinical psychologists in turn, all hidden from view by a screen. The patient is able to select which psychologist they feel most comfortable with and then they spend a day together somewhere relaxing and away from the Institute. So far, results have had limited success but Dr Pepsi is optimistic and one day 'hopes to buy a hat'. Perhaps the final word should go to Mr Jooooooones:

'One day I'd like to be cured and lead a normal life. If you were to be cured and lead a normal life, how would you be cured and what normal life would you lead and why? That goes to number two.'

Q: What did James Bond say when he was poorly and someone suggested going to seek medical assistance and he didn't want to?

A: Doctor No

Q: What did the Timelord say when he was poorly and someone suggested going to seek medical assistance from someone with a rather outlandish name?

A: Doctor Who

Q: What did the song that goes 'ting tang willa willa bing bong' say when it was poorly and someone suggested going to seek medical assistance from a green woman in a black pointy hat?

A: Witch (which) Doctor

Q: What do you call a feline two (or four)-fingered chocolate biscuit wearing a football strip?

A: Kit Cat

I'd probably better stop now. I can imagine that a few sides have already been split. Go and see a doctor immediately.

Bit Of a Dark Rug – A Poem

What has gone wrong?
My mind is going ding-dong
I sigh and shrug
I've got a bit of a dark rug

I start to cry
I ask myself, why?
I've been such a mug
I've bought a bit of a dark rug

Should I take it back?
It's giving me a heart attack
Lift it up, give it a tug
Good bye, bit of a dark rug.

Happy Birthday to Sher-bee (me)

Tributes have arrived in their thousands from around the world to celebrate the first birthday of 'The World of Sherby57'. They have come via letter, fax, carrier pigeon and wise man.

Hundreds of jubilant fans blocked Sherby57 Plaza as they attempted to express their gratitude via the medium of a candle-light vigil. This was a bit silly because it was in the day time and the candles weren't that effective in the glaring sun, but the sentiment was there nonetheless.

Meanwhile, a cavalcade of A-listers, from the worlds of entertainment, sport and business, jetted in for an exclusive cocktail party at one of Warrington's most prestigious nightspots. It's been a crazy time.

As the festivities finally draw to a close, all the staff at Sherby57 would love to thank our fans for making this first year possible. Yes, we'd love to thank you, but, of course, we can't actually do that. I mean, come on, it's all been down to us, hasn't it? It should really be you lot thanking us, shouldn't it? Yes? Well, I'm glad we cleared that up.

Let's hope that the next year brings equal success!

Bon Voyage!

Simon Cowell: Dream Smasher

How does Simon Cowell influence the war for reality?

It's a simple answer with no question.

Within some circles (and other shapes), Simon Cowell is known as The Dream Smasher. Circles within the circles (like a social Venn diagram) argue about whether this is a positive or negative role to play. Some say that by crushing people's dreams Cowell is destroying the dream energy of those poor unfortunates and is causing a disintegration of the shared memetic field.

Others argue that by putting a stop to unachievable goals, he is actually freeing up their inner mental jizz-fluid to launch a full-scale ejaculation on the frontal meme-sphere.

They're all idiots. The War is much more complex than that. Not only is there not a good side or a bad side, there are actually no sides at all. There's no floor and there's definitely not a roof. When you actually stop and analyse the facts, you'll realise that there's not even a war occurring at all. Despite knowing this, me and my colleagues fight our battles every day. As I say, it's quite complex.

Understandably, people struggle with this concept. I know I do and I'm deeply embroiled within it all. It's fair to say that this eternal struggle for comprehension is a key component of the war\non-war.

Stick with me, my children, and all will become clear. Only it probably won't.

A Joke I Was Once Told

I was once told a cracking joke by someone at work. It was one of those jokes that is all in the telling, so I'll endeavor to recreate it word for word. Here we go:

Well the first thing you need to know is that Lye is a small town in the Black Country and it's situated somewhere between Stourbridge and Dudley. The other thing you need to know is that in the Black Country, instead of saying 'I am', they say 'Yam'.

Now, bearing that in mind, what do you call a Chinese man who is somewhere between Stourbridge and Dudley?

Yam in Lye.

It really is the way you tell 'em.

Hallo!

Ich bin Hans Klaussner, and you may be remembering me from my previous emissions when I am introducing myself to you and also from when I am talking about my skills as a dishwasher. I am hoping that you have now been fully reminisced and are able to input my new ideas. Danke.

In the multitude of days full of regret since we have last been speaking, old Hansy has been promoted to the magnificent position of head washer dishes. It is moment of maximum adulation for my Momma and Poppa and we are all overcome with lashings of Teutonic pride. Ja, Momma und Poppa have indeed come to Eng-land to stay in my bed of sits and we will imminently commence our festivities. Is 'real hot potato' as you crazy Brits is saying.

With sadness, I must report that Herr Klaussner (that is being one-self), is still without ladylove within mine domain. I wish with most sincerity that I am meeting England Rose, the proponent of beauty in my life. Last week, I was attending speed-date evening with my good friend Cheface (the chef), and you will have wished us the best of bloody British, what what! Spit spot! Alas, you are not able to make luck travel back in time and we did not meet a suitable lady. I am still looking and am happy to go on a date without Cheface. He is something of a burden for one such as myself, but do not please be telling him of what I say.

Bitte. I am now commencing my informing of you of my further plans. Poppa Klaussner, he is being my Vater, is using many Euro to pay for my vacation with Uncle Sam of the U of SA! Ja, you better believe it buddy, Hans is coming to get you. My excitement has come to the top of my brim and it is already spilling over onto my new jeans. It's a little messy but Hans can cope!

I am beginning my tour with New Yorkshire within but a few hours and I am hoping to be scoffing the New Yorkshire pudding (mit gravy!) at the top of Das Empire Strikes Building. In the words of our American cousins 'Git your butt out of the place and lick my balls.' At least this is what I am thinking they are going to be saying. I have not watched too many of the American film and so I am guessing from things that Cheface says in the restaurant.

Alas, I must trot as I have a monoplane to embark upon. My bags are packed and I am most ready to go. Who knows what adventures may lurk in those most united of states. Hans simply cannot be imagining such things. As a compromise, I am hoping that I am keeping you complete with my updates once I have set foot in said country. In the words of my Momma 'Help me help you.'

As always, brimming with man-love,

Hans

Toast Me – A Poem

Fluffy white innards

Tempting my soul

Sliced whole, like my love

Where does it come from?

Why do I need it?

These questions go unanswered

As I watch you burn

The crust is a layer

A boundary between realities

The mechanical jaws tease me

Spread my erotic butter

I am denied

The toast no more

No more

Documentaries, of one kind or another, are all over the television schedules this week. We start at the more educational end of the spectrum as we take a look **Inside the Institute** (Monday). This fascinating series of films gives us unprecedented access to Warrington's prestigious Torben Piechnik Institute, one of the most lauded research facilities in the Western world. Not content to study boring areas like the origins of the universe and a cure for cancer, the TPI have branched out into areas such a banana-penised men, Blind Date based speech disorders, flying pigs and pegs on widges.

This week's episode follows head of the institute, Dr Glen Medeiros, and his quest to link missing socks to the fractal nature of the universe. It's pretty technical stuff and is pretty incomprehensible to the lay viewer. Luckily, Dr. Medeiros has such a lovely singing voice that you'll soon forgive him for all the scientific jargon. We see a different side to the great scientist in a touching scene in which the Doc visits long-term patient "Mr Banana-Penis" in his Devon retreat. I challenge anyone not to shed a tear when the two men are reunited.

It might be a stretch to describe the next show as a documentary, but I must. Those who remember *Celebrity Chip Shop* will be shocked by the blatant plagiarism of **Celeb Kebab House** (every bloody night). The format is exactly the same: two teams of "celebrities" run rival fast food outlets with the winners being the ones who make the most profit.   At the time of writing, I've only seen the first couple of episodes, but it's as bad as you might imagine. Only a hell of a lot worse. Celebrity-based reality shows have chewed up and spat out just about all the Z-listers willing to appear. This has meant that the producers of CKH have had to find a layer of celebrity lower than Z. The contestants include: the guy off the "Astonish" infomercial from the early 90's, a woman who won a competition to meet Take That backstage at a concert, someone who once auditioned for boy band "A1", Jeremy Spake's next-door neighbour and Edd The Duck. The series is saved from complete disaster by the inclusion of radio superstar Dave "The Rave" Burley. It's a mystery why a broadcaster of Burley's calibre would agree to be part of this show, but we're all mightily glad that he has. In the second episode, we see the DJ deal with a tricky customer by singing him a lullaby. It's an unusual approach, but it certainly does the trick. All in all, it's going to be a rubbish programme, but we'll all end up watching it anyway.

Last, but not least, for this week is the groundbreaking, **The History of Ring Binders** (Sunday). In this first episode of a twenty part series, we learn of the humble beginnings of the ring binder in the days before paper was invented. In these troubling times, many ring binders were forced to eke a living through prostitution, and the programme makers do not pull any punches in the graphic description of those harrowing times. This week concludes with the invention of papyrus in 2000BC and the emancipation of the original Egyptian ring binders. It's truly uplifting.

Richie Cunningham's Hair

Over the weekend, I had something of a countdown conundrum that I was mulling over. I couldn't decide whether Richie Cunningham was truly a ginger or if his head was actually a holographic representation of Satan (original evil). I spent a fruitless couple of hours googling for an answer, but even the mighty G has its limits. I don't want to sound like I'm overreacting but it seemed that the whole future of the universe hung on the solution to this interminable riddle, and so I knew that I had to travel to another plane of existence in search of satisfaction.

I briskly donned my ceremonial thong and cape and adopted the infamously tricky 'Pomegranate Position'. With the smell of incense and freshly fried chips combining mystically in my nostrils, I began to sink deeper and deeper in to a meditative trance. As something of an expert, it takes only 4-5 hours to reach my spiritual plateau from which I can commune with my spirit guide, former Wimbledon goalkeeper, Hans Segers. Obviously, the real Hans Segers isn't dead or anything. This is just the form that my spirit guide has chosen to take. Don't ask me why, it's all very mysterious.

After filling Hans in on my reasons for visiting, he suggested that the best way to find the answers that I was seeking was to create a mock-universe based loosely on *The Kids of Degrassi Street*. Again, I have no idea why this was the appropriate solution, I've just come to trust Hans over the years. Anyway, he did most of the work and soon he had mentally knocked-up a reasonably well functioning universe. There were a few too many features from *Degrassi Junior High* for my liking, but beggars can't be choosers.

Hans insisted that this next portion of my quest must be performed alone. After kissing him tenderly on both cheeks, I gracefully floated skywards in my astral form. It definitely beats walking. I swooped over the terrifying landscape like a crazy man-eagle, hoping and praying for answers. I hunted high and low, very much in the style of A-Ha, without ever really knowing what I was looking for. I felt utterly defeated; it was proving more fruitless than my initial googling.

Then, as I flew high above the rooftops, I spotted a sliver speck far below, seemingly winking at me. Intrigued, I descended with haste towards the glistening metallic mystery. Alas, it was some kind of elaborate trap as before I could even reach it, I found myself enveloped in a cosmic napsack! How I wish that Hans Segers had been there with me.

After my initial panic subsided, I began to get my bearings and began to explore. I trod carefully up and down the napsack looking for some sort of clue to what I should do next. It was then that I heard a booming voice coming from, seemingly, all around me.

'Go low, yet go high whist though roam, young warrior, though beating breast may yet send sense through reason.'

'What the frig does that mean?' I humbly replied.

No answer was forthcoming, instead there was a blinding flash of light, and, when it subsided, a being strongly resembling Wizbit was stood before my very eyes.

'I am not Wizbit,' said he, somehow knowing what I was thinking. 'I am your own mind connecting directly to the universe. Believe it or not, your quest is at an end, you already know the answers of which you seek.'

Before I had chance to tell the Wizbit look-alike that his answer was awfully glib, I found myself being pulled back towards the physical realm. I landed with a thud and when I opened my eyes I was back in my living room. My thong and cape were completely drenched in sweat and I was panting like dog that had been forced to run a marathon for charity.

As I lay back on the sofa, stewing in my own juices, I realised that, of course, I knew the answer.

He really is just a ginger.

And with that, I went to make a brew.

I'm really not having a good week. I don't care what people tell you, it's definitely not easy being an existential warrior. Over the last few weeks I've been completely and utterly bombarded with pointless psychic attacks. They're the mystical equivalent of spam e-mails. Very annoying. In a desperate attempt to get some respite, I'm currently holed up in a secret, psychically-shielded location. All I'll say is that I'm freezing my arse off in an igloo somewhere in South America.

Luckily, I'm not alone. I'm in the process of warming myself up with my companion\concubine Bontempi, by snuggling up under our pile of furs. Oh yeah, baby, we've gone old school on your asses.

Our supposedly safe haven has been under attack by negative orbs for the last 3 earth days and, frankly, it's left us both drained. My aura has literally never been so weak. As a result, I've been reduced to spewing utterances such as: 'Me want me tea, me hun-gree Bom Tempy.'

Bontempi can only grunt in reply; she's even worse than me.

Thankfully, the worst of it seems to be over and I have felt a 12% increase in my qi, even since I started writing this. Rest assured that normal service will be resumed shortly. There's only so much igloo that one man can take.

A Hilarious A-Team Joke

My friend has been feeling down lately, so I popped round to see how he was doing. I found him sat on the floor drawing a stretched out portrait of Dirk Benedict. I said to him: 'Hey, why the long Face?'

Editor's Note: This joke caused shock-waves in the world of comedy when it was originally published in October 2008. It was reported in several newspapers that three people had died because they had laughed so hard at the joke, but these claims were never substantiated. I'm proud to report that the joke was the worthy recipient of the 2009 Nobel Prize for Humour. Dirk Benedict was present to collect the honour on behalf of the Sherby57 Foundation. In his acceptance speech, Mr Benedict quizzically pointed at a Cylon that was stood behind him on stage. Everybody laughed their socks off. Literally.

Hey Gang!

I imagine that you're all collecting firewood in preparation for next week's festive Bonfire Evening! Gosh, it's my favourite bank holiday of the year, as we all remember the day that Guy Siner left Allo Allo. This date, coincidentally, also marks the last ever episode of Allo Allo.

Anyway, in honour of the 5th December, I have written this poem:

Bonfire Night

Bonfire Night!

Everybody's happy

We all feel right

Let's make a fire

Stoke it real hot

Here's Lieutenant Gruber

In his little tank

Throw him on the fire

And eat a jacket spud

It's not the best poem, to be fair. Bonfire night has the habit of bringing out the worst in me.

It's time, once again, for me to take my fishing rod of criticism and cast it deep into the lake of television. Let's hope that I will catch the tench of good programming.

It's hard to believe that it's been twenty years since **The Brothers Greenthumb** (Sunday) first hit our screens. I'm happy to say that the old girl is still going strong as it makes its welcome return for a new series. The everyday story of a family of gardeners has changed dramatically in the last two decades. The overarching plot of the first series revolved around eldest brother Alan's battle with a fungal foot infection and its effect on his ability to strim. Those simple times are long gone. The latest episode follows on directly from last year's gory cliffhanger. Will Alan's son, Skags, survive the bitter turf war with their arch-enemies the Lawnbusters? Will Cherry recover from the multiple gunshot wounds inflicted by a disgruntled customer? Has Cedric really managed to overcome his heroin addiction or will he be back down to the potting shed with his works? I won't spoil it for you, just make sure that you're tuned in for this unmissable hour of television.

Controversial game show **Fear My Clit** (Wednesday) continues with more husbands being humiliated by their wives as they use their empowered vaginas to hypnotise their spouses to commit a series of demeaning acts. This week follows the Smith-Jones, and features scenes such as Mr Smith-Jones licking a wellington boot in a bridal shop, crying over some spilled milk and vomiting into the postman's sack. It's weirder than anything on Japanese TV, and it could seriously damage your mental health.

Finally, there's the resurgent **Peabody Place** (Monday, Tuesday – 2 episodes, Wednesday, Thursday, Friday - 3 episodes, Saturday, Sunday omnibus), which has another barnstorming week lined up for us. The alien invasion storyline continues apace as Bill Bollington organises the resistance into an effective fighting unit and they finally capture their first Oooong. Will they manage to get the plans to the mother-ship from the amphibian extraterrestrial? Elsewhere, Beryl considers her options as the credit crunch bites and she loses her job at the biscuit factory.

Show Me Magic – A Poem

There was a man
Whose life was tragic
He said to God
"Show me magic!"
He listened closely
His answer missed
God chuckled quietly
"I don't exist!"

10. Sherby57 melts in your hand, not in your mouth.

9. The first galaxy to be conquered by Sherby57 was Alpha Omicron Pi 12.

8. The first rule of Sherby57 is you don't blink unless you need to.

7. Monkeys can sense when Sherby57 is angry.

6. Sherby57 is not responsible for the credit crunch, despite what Kanye West might think.

5. The second rule of Sherby57 is wipe your feet before entry.

4. Sherby57 is made entirely out of pine cones, except for the bits that aren't.

3. Many countries are named after Sherby57, including France, Botswana and Iceland.

2. Sherby57 is an anagram of 'large toad infestation'.

1. There are only nine unknown facts about Sherby57.

In an upsetting turn of events, it has emerged that there will be no post published on 'The World of Sherby57' today. In an official statement for the web-site, lawyer turned farmer, George Ofdejungle, said the following:

"We hereby regretfully inform the general public that today, the tenth of December, in the year of our Lord (Screaming Lord Sutch) two thousand and eight, that there will be no entry on the blog cum web-site, hereby and furthermore, known as "The World of Sherby57", or Sherby57 as it is more commonly known. It's just a bit easier. This decision has not come easily and has left many of the company's staff heartbroken, morally bankrupt and\or illegally immigrated. We hope that you will support us through this difficult time."

Skeptics, including Dr. Glen Madeiros of the prestigious Torben Piechnik Institute, believe that this itself constitutes a post, and as such the announcement should be ignored.

If you have a problem, and no one else can help, I'm sure you'd be tempted to call the A-Team. This would be a mistake on many levels, but mainly because they're entirely fictional. No, if you really want help, there is only one man for the job. That man is the Masked Avenger.

With his jolly orange mask and his vampiric teeth, he has the dual abilities of soothing the innocent and terrifying the guilty. He fights for what's right, what's tight and what's slight. He's very even handed.

Yes, the Masked Avenger is Warrington's latest (and arguably greatest) costumed crimefighter. Does he actually have any powers? Are those vampire teeth real or just some cheap plastic ones that came out of a cracker? How does he keep his mask so shiny? None of these questions truly matter. All you need to know is that he's keeping the streets safer for you and your kin.

The one pertinent question that does arise is: who is the man behind the mask? Perhaps we'll never know. But, sometimes we need a little mystery in this mundane world that we laughingly call 'the world'. If the sight of the Masked Avenger bounding over Warrington's famous skyline can't provide this mystery for us, I don't know what can.

FIREHEART!

Johnny Fireheart reached into the pocket of his expensive sheepskin jacket and pulled out his car keys. As he tossed them into the air he couldn't help but admire his pristine, black Ford Capri: a gift from his exotic lover Choo-Choo LaTrain. With its sleek lines and shiny bonnet, it was much more than just a car. To Johnny it was a symbol. It was a Capri that purred like a kitten when treated nicely but roared like a lion when angered. It was a Capri that had too many miles on the clock, but was too tough to even care. It was a Capri that had seen the black side of the road and had escaped with not even a loose chipping in a tyre tread. Just like Johnny.

He slid himself forcibly into the luxurious leather driver's seat and looked at himself in the rear-view mirror. He liked what he saw and told himself so. 'You look so fucking hot tonight, Johnny,' said Johnny. Fireheart ran his hand through his slicked back hair and chuckled, he was ready to roll. Well, almost ready. He reached over to the glove compartment and retrieved his trademark black sunglasses. It was only when they were slipped firmly over his chiselled visage that he felt truly ready. He was Johnny Fireheart. It didn't matter to Johnny that it was 10 o'clock and it was pitch black outside, he always wore the shades when driving. This reckless policy had even lead to a few deaths, but it was important to maintain an image. Twirling his keys between his muscular fingers, he sensuously slid the key deep into the ignition and turned; the mighty engine started with a satisfying growl. Johnny's foot twitched deep within his expensive crocodile-skin shoes, desperate to rev his magnificent machine. But he restrained himself. The Capri needed to be treated just right, treated like a lady. The sole of his shoe caressed the accelerator pedal and teasingly began to pump, softly at first, then growing harder and longer, pumping until you could almost hear the engine begging him to stop. Then, just as the glistening auto-mobile thought that she could take no more, Johnny dropped the handbrake and dumped the clutch. The Capri's tyres squealed in ecstasy as he pulled away in a plume of oily black smoke; the molten tyres leaving thick black marks on the road like the devil's mascara.

As he thundered along the grimy streets, Johnny took time to assess the day's events. He had risen around noon, hung over and aching from a brawl the previous evening. Needless to say, his opponents were feeling much worse. Not having a traditional job, Johnny failed to keep traditional work hours. It was almost three in the afternoon when he decided to leave the flat; a bolt hole he kept just for occasions when he needed to lie low or just fancied a brew. He made his usual rounds, keeping in touch with the various contacts, freaks and perverts that kept him in business. It had been a relatively uneventful day, and he was already mentally running a bubble bath and debating whether to open that expensive Merlot or stick with a simple Blue Nun for his post soak relaxation. Before he could get to that, he had one more job to do and he grimaced as he reached his last stop of the day – Ken's Key Kutters.

The locksmith's wasn't really a locksmith's; it was merely a front for a two-bit sherbet fiddler called Panda Pete. He was neither a panda nor called Pete. There was also nobody called Ken involved. It was all very confusing. Johnny forcefully entered the shop and as he strode through the door a little bell tinkled, alerting Panda Pete to his presence. The two men looked at each other: Johnny with disgust, Panda Pete with awe.

'Johnny, Johnny! My old friend! How the devil is one?' slimed the cretinous criminal.

'You're no friend of mine, Panda. I'd barely even call you a pal. But as you're asking: I'm angry. Angry that I have to see your toad-like gob again. Now, where's my money?'

Panda Pete gulped and a single drop of fearful sweat slowly trickled down his aardvark-like nose. Johnny waited impatiently until the droplet reached the fetid tip of the bulbous protuberance and dropped pitifully to the dusty lino. Johnny took a menacing step closer and ground the sweat-drop into the dust with the heel of his shoe. 'I won't ask again, Panda,' he growled.

'Johnny, please! I don't have the money here, but I do have it for you. One of my associates has it. He told me you could pick it up from here.' He handed Johnny an envelope. It was quite a fancy one like you might get at some awards ceremony. Johnny raised a sardonic eyebrow. This had better be good. He roughly opened the paper sheath and shook free its contents. A small business card fell in to his hand. It simply read 'Club Tropicana'.

Interesting, very interesting.

Johnny couldn't believe that The Lips could be involved with a scuzzball like Panda Pete, but, then again, Greater Londonbury was a crazy kind of town.

'It looks as though you have a stay of execution,' snarled Fireheart. 'But if I find out that this isn't on the level I'm going to come back here, grab a handful of keys – ones for mortice locks, not those tiny yale type - and I'm going to ram them so far up you that you'll be setting off airport metal detectors until you're seventy.' With this, he span around balletically and flounced from the grotty emporium.

Now, here he was, driving his throbbing motor towards the club. In fact, he spent so long thinking about the reasons why he was driving to the club, that he had actually driven past it some time ago. As he regained his potent wits, he cursed and slammed on his breaks, dramatically spinning the gleaming machine in the opposite direction (simultaneously scaring retired school teacher Norman Bradley, who was behind Johnny in his Vauxhall Nova, in to proclaiming 'ruddy hooligan'. This was the most naughty swear that Norman had ever done. Johnny had this effect on people). It took Fireheart mere moments before he was back outside the infamous nightspot and he found a secluded alley in which to park the Capri. He threw a ten pound note at a tramp and gave the vagrant a look which said 'protect my car or I will give you a colostomy with a plastic fork', and walked to the street. It was time to meet his fate.

The light flickered outside Club Tropicana; it was a dive. Johnny knew it, Choo-Choo knew it and so did most of the low-lives that lived in the bustling metropolis known as Greater Londonbury. The club was situated on Doctor Dre Lane, renowned throughout the borough for its myriad of watering holes and dance venues. They all played the same shit music and served four shots for a fiver. 'God,' said Johnny, running his fingers through his greasy black hair. 'I hate this town.'

It was perhaps his foul mood that prevented him from noticing how suspiciously quiet the street was, even for a Tuesday. By rights, his Fireheart-Sense should be tingling, but in his current state of mind he just strode towards the main entrance like a big, tough cowboy. It was important that he conveyed the correct body language as he approached the bouncers, Biff and Quentin.

Biff and Quentin were the most infamous doormen in the town and their reputation was richly deserved. One of them was a bruiser, an uneducated thug with the body of an ape and the brain of a walnut; he could pulp yams just by looking at them. The other was a cad, an Eton educated thespian who was fluent in the ancient language of pain; he reportedly once carved the entire works of Oscar Wilde onto an enemy's face using an uncoiled paper clip. I bet you've picked which one of these men is which, but you'd be wrong. Yes, Quentin is the bruiser and Biff is the cad. You should know by now that Greater Londonbury is one fucked up town.

'Hi,' said Johnny, giving a little growl that told the two bruisers that they had better watch themselves. 'How are you feeling tonight?' The three men shared a glance (although they didn't share a moment, that would just be weird) as they all weighed each other up. The goons knew that Johnny was a master at several martial arts and that he always kept nunchucks tucked into his argyle socks. He wasn't a man to be trifled with.

'I'm a bit down actually, Johnny.' replied Quentin. Biff quickly cut him off with a stern look which told the perspiring primate that he would do the talking.

'We're absolutely spiffing, Johnny, thanks ever so much for asking. How is life treating you, old bean?'

'I'm like Tony The Tiger, Biff, I'm Grrrrreat,' joked Johnny. Biff laughed nervously. Quentin didn't get it at all. He was still obsessed by the Honey Monster and so had never tried Frosties. 'Anyway, boys, it's time I went and saw your boss.' With this, Johnny marched into the foyer. As he went, Biff could barely suppress a knowing grin from his noble face.

Johnny nodded at Tina, the cloakroom assistant. She was a nice enough girl but he wouldn't leave his prized denim jacket with her. It had once belonged to Shakin' Stevens, and Johnny had survived a frenzied bidding war to get it. It was only when he had passed Tina and entered the main room of the club that Johnny realised that something was out of place: there was nobody else there.

Almost nobody.

He looked over towards the bar and sat at a stool was Luca 'Bobby The Lips' Burloni. He was the owner of the club and not uncoincidentally he was also the local mafia boss. He was also the man that Johnny was here to see. Fireheart had dealt with Luca in the past and one thing was for sure, somebody always died. Johnny couldn't help but wonder whether this time it could be his turn.

Burloni was a fat, bald man wearing an ill-fitting but expensive suit and he sat alone at the bar, eating pasta from a bowl. He had a napkin tucked into the front of his shirt to catch the badly aimed ragu. He occasionally used the napkin to dab sweat from his wrinkled brow. This was a pointless task as his head was so damp that it gleamed from the neon light above him. He was nothing if he wasn't a living, breathing stereotype. Upon hearing footsteps behind him, the corpulent criminal swivelled on his stool and greeted the oncoming Johnny with a smile. 'So, Johnny, you're finally here.'

'YEAH!' shouted Johnny. He didn't intend to let The Lips intimidate him and so was overly aggressive in his opening gambit.

Johnny took a cigarette from the packet he had stashed in his top pocket and lit up. Fuck the smoking ban and fuck Luca Burloni.

'Johnny, Johnny, there's no need for the attitude. We're all friends here.' Burloni looked like a cat playing with a mouse. Sadly for him, Johnny Fireheart was not a mouse.

'I'm not here to play pattacake with my friends, Luca. I'm here because Panda Pete says you have my money. If that's not true then I'll be on my way.' Johnny didn't want to be in this place any longer that was absolutely necessary. By the look on Burloni's face, he sensed that things could go very wrong. Burloni held his hands up and pretended to look like he was shocked by Johnny's abruptness.

'Johnny, we've know each other for many years, and I know you as a man. The lowly amount that Panda Pete owes is beneath the contempt of a man such as you. A man such as us. I have something much more lucrative for you,' he paused dramatically. 'I have a job for you.'

Fireheart scratched his crotch and let out a subsonic growl directed directly at the obese Cosa Nostra leader. He could feel the cold tendrils of fate inexorably pulling him into the quicksand of doom. It was a feeling that he didn't like one iota.

'What kind of job? I don't work for your kind any more,' retorted Fireheart. Burloni stood up and approached Johnny. He got close, closer than close. He got closer than you ever could imagine. Johnny battled to maintain consciousness as he became overwhelmed by the pungent garlicky breath of the grotesque gangster. Burloni gave his answer:

'I want you to steal my mother.'

Johnny dropped his cigarette to floor.

Johnny was reeling and he staggered from the club as though drunk, even thought he wasn't. He'd only just about managed to gulp down a pint of orange and soda with Burloni. His mouth had become very dry when he'd heard the proposition. Somehow, Fireheart managed to compose himself as he passed the doormen and even gave them his customary snarl. They both instinctively took a step back. It was good to know that he still had it.

Johnny reached the alleyway and placed his hands on the shiny roof of the Capri. He took a huge deep breath and tried to gather his thoughts. It took him a minute or two to realise that the hobo was looking at him expectantly. He scanned the car before giving his verdict: 'You did good, kid.' The tramp smiled in gratitude as Johnny opened the car door and slid onto the snug leather seat. He snapped his leather driving gloves on and started the engine. His driving style wasn't as aggressive now, he knew it had its time and place, and this was neither the time nor the place. And so he wasn't.

He cruised the mean streets of Greater Londonbury with no particular destination in mind. But that wasn't the point; the Capri was where Johnny always went to think. He splashed and crashed through the many dirty puddles and smoked cigarette after cigarette as he pondered Burloni's offer. An offer that wasn't so much an offer as it was a threat. And Johnny knew that when Luca Burloni made a threat then it wasn't a threat; it was a promise. It all made Johnny's head swirl, which was swirling enough with all the nicotine pumping through his central nervous system. He was usually an animal of instinct and that instinct invariably proved correct. He once had bitten off the nose of a man just because of the way he whistled when he walked into a bar. Even some of Johnny's nastier associates thought he had gone mad. He hadn't. The man had a gun concealed in his right nostril. It was just one of the many incidents that had made his reputation as the town's number one 'go-to-guy'. His razor sharp instincts were telling him two things about Burloni's proposal: he shouldn't take the job and he had no choice but to take it.

By the time he came to the conclusion that he had no choice, it was beginning to get light outside. It was late, too damned late. With the adrenaline and nicotine subsiding within his honed cerebral cortex, he was suddenly overcome with tiredness. He'd been driving for hours and he needed a bed, and he needed it now. Johnny never looked his best without his beauty sleep, and Johnny always liked to look his best. There was only one obvious choice; he'd go and see Choo-Choo. She always had a kind word for him, and when the kind word didn't work she had a very talented tongue.

The Capri screeched to a halt outside the house. All the lights were off. But then it was the middle of the night so she'd obviously be in bed. Johnny reached the front door and spat on the ground out of habit. He could taste the stale cigarette smoke in his sputum and needed to wash it away with a large Scotch. He grimaced to himself as he looked under the plant pot to find the spare key. When would she learn that this town isn't safe, Johnny thought to himself. Choo-Choo may have been an incredibly erotic lover, but she didn't have a grasp of basic home safety. She wouldn't even get a smoke alarm and he feared that one day she was going to pay. 'Fire kills in minutes, smoke kills in seconds,' he grumbled under his breath, before slotting the key into the lock as smoothly as he shortly hoped to be slotting into Choo-Choo.

He strode purposefully into the hall way. He thought he had been quiet but he had disturbed Choo-Choo's magnificent pet parrot, Sir Walter Pilkington-Smythe, who squawked to life. Johnny sneaked into the kichenette and retrieved the bottle of single malt that he kept secreted in the bread bin. He took a giant glug straight from the bottle and wiped his mouth on his sleeve. Just like in the movies. He took another long slurp from the dwindling bottle to ready himself either for sleep or frantic love-making. Feeling fully prepared for his immediate fate, Johnny began to climb the stairs.

'Who's a pretty boy, then?' said Sir Walter Pilkington-Smythe.

'I am,' growled Johnny. At the top of the stairs, he paused before pushing open the door to the exotic boudoir. Choo-Choo was awake. And naked. Her succulent flower glistened in the soft light and seemed to be winking at Johnny. His mouth began to water, as simultaneously, his proud member began to stiffen like a fireman's hose becoming engorged with water.

'It's about time you got here,' said Choo-Choo with a smirk. 'I'm wetter than Warrington Walking Day down there.' Johnny looked at her and liked what he saw. Choo-Choo was slender, tanned and toned like a race horse. Her long, blonde tresses tumbled down her back and seemed to frame her exquisite bosom. Her breasts were naturally full, and seemed to float like lilies in a pond. She had a dragon tattooed down the full length of her left leg that was so detailed that it had taken nearly a thousand hours to complete. She didn't have the heart to tell the tattooist that she had actually asked for a tattoo of a wagon. Most importantly, for Johnny, she was fully shaven.

'Time for supper,' laughed Johnny, as he slipped off his t-shirt and jeans to reveal a toned, muscular, hairy body, and a cock so hard that it looked like a flag pole on the side of a skyscraper. 'And I want to eat a big slice of pussy pie.' He crossed the room with intent, and knew right then that he wasn't going to get much sleep that night.

Johnny tossed and turned in the sweaty bed after consuming Choo-Choo's sensual body like a lion devouring a wildebeest. His lover was asleep, she snored loudly, and he could faintly hear the squawking of Sir Walter Pilkington-Smythe. Despite his lack of sleep, Johnny was restless, and decided to use the time to ponder everything he knew about Burloni's mother.

Everyone knew that Mamma Burloni was ancient, but nobody knew her actual age. Some rumours that Johnny had heard suggested that she was over 70 when she gave birth to Luca. This would have made her present age well over a ton. Under normal circumstances, Johnny would dismiss such speculation as obvious bullshit, but with Mamma Burloni you could never be sure. She was well know for being wizened with age, some people said that her head was the size of a large conker and just as shiny. Johnny had met the formidable matriarch on several occasions and knew that this was only a slight exaggeration. Being exceptionally well connected in the town, Fireheart did know more than most about Mamma's history. She was born on the small Italian island of Sizzleonia, a hot bed of mafia activity, and was known as Mamma from childhood with no one really knowing why. If she ever had another name then nobody is left alive who remembers it, not even herself. As she grew older she blossomed in to a beautiful young lady, often ostracised by those jealous of her natural grace and good looks. She spent a solitary life with her parents, quietly tending to their gerbil farm. They were poor but blissfully happy with their precious gerbils. As she reached the age of consent, stories began to circle the island of the angelic girl who sold gerbils at the local market. Soon it became impossible for her to visit the market due to the large number of admirers that came to stare at her endlessly. Indeed, she could barely sell any gerbils as she was inundated with love letters and flowers. Men became frantic in their attempts to woo her and it soon escalated into bloody violence. Many men tragically died. Sizzleonia was declared a war-zone for over three years as every single man on the island fought for her hand in marriage (even the ones that were already married). The male populace was sent mad with desire.

The matter was finally settled when Big Poppa Luigi Burloni stepped down from his small fishing boat onto the Sizzleonian shore. He was not a native of the island, but was well known to the local fisherman as the most vital man on the high seas. It was unknown where he actually came from and some said that he was actually born on his boat, The Salty Pearl. Luigi had avoided the island for the 3 years of the war, but something drew him in on that fateful day. Those who were in the immediate vicinity of his landing dropped their weapons in shock, they had never seen him on land before and it was almost too much for their minds to comprehend. Once on land, Luigi let out a mighty roar that was so loud that it drowned out the sound of Mount Etna erupting and it was so frightening that all fighting stopped immediately. Luigi Burloni strode like a king over the corpses in search of the fabled beauty; he knew of her through pure animal instinct and had not heard any of the tales of sweet Mamma. Men, women, and children fell to their knees as he traversed the dusty roads, getting ever closer to the humble farm. As he approached the tumbledown shack that Mamma's family called a home, the sky turned blood red. The meeting of such elemental forces made even Mother Nature tremble. Luigi removed his hat and opened the door of the ramshackle dwelling, drawn inexorably to his fate.

Electricity crackled in the air of the hut, and the chemistry between the pair was so potent that Mamma's mother and father immediately melted into a puddle of gloop. The lovers looked into each others eyes for the first, and only, time, and moved towards each other. They instinctively knew that they were now man and wife, bound together forever, no matter what happened. They gently reached out for each other, but as their fingertips touched there was an almighty explosion and they were thrown, scattered across the globe. Every peasant within a 5 mile radius was instantly killed.

Luigi found himself alone and naked somewhere in the Australian outback. As soon as he regained his senses and had quenched his thirst in a local billabong, he began his quest to find his true love. He roamed the earth calling 'Mamma Mamma, where are you?' for years and years to no avail. His journey only ended in the 1950s, when, after a convoluted set of circumstances, he became the first Italian in space (preceding the more famous American and Russian efforts by a full decade). Becoming embroiled in an attack by the evil

KwahKwahKawh army from the planet Bizunginddunflopflipflopplipplopplow, he risked his life to save the human race. Eventually he sacrificed his love of Mamma to take the throne of the Great Parp to become King Big Poppa Luigi, the First of the Holy ZizzJizzMizzLizzPubQuiz Empire in order to bring peace to the galaxy (but that really is a story in its own right, it's not really totally relevant for Johnny's purposes).

Mamma Burloni resurfaced many years later in a seedy part of Greater Londonbury, pregnant with Luigi's child. The traumatic events has transformed her from a fair maiden into a being of pure evil. The prolonged pregnancy resulted in her emitting a heady cocktail of pheromones and hormones that gave her effective control over any man, but had robbed her of her transcendent beauty. With her new found ability she quickly built a criminal empire, and a chain of chippys for tax purposes. Many years later she gave birth to Luca, who emerged from her womb as a fully grown man. They clashed before he could suck his first drop of milk from her motherly teat. However, she believed in keeping your enemies (and children) close and Luca rapidly rose to be her right hand man. It was around this time that Johnny himself first met Mamma when he completed a job for her that he was not proud of. It was at the same time as that job that the bitter feud between Luca and Mamma began in earnest.

As he lay sweating in Choo-Choo's bed, Johnny came to realise that perhaps the two events were linked. Maybe, if he hadn't taken that job from Mamma all those years ago, then he wouldn't be in his current predicament. He knew that if he was going to get out of stealing Mamma then he knew he would have to revisit the events that started the ball rolling.

It was early. Too damned early for Johnny; he'd woken up almost before he'd gone to sleep. Luckily, with his panther-like reflexes he was almost dangerously alert. He took a long last draw from his menthol Superking and flicked the butt. It was at that precise moment that he knew he should have wound the window down. Now there was ash on the floor of the Capri and Johnny's crotch was on fire. Well, it wouldn't be the first time, he thought to himself. Part of him had wished that he'd stayed in Choo-Choo's warm embrace a little longer. He was also gutted that he was going to miss Jeremy Kyle. He shrugged to himself; he had enough problems of his own to solve.

Johnny glared through the windscreen at "The Thyme, The Plaice", Mamma Burloni's flag ship chip shop. He hoped that its evocative piscine-related exterior would help jog his memory. It was only half past six in the A.M. and the Chippy wouldn't open for another forty five minutes for the early morning rush. Johnny could never understand how builders could eat so much greasy food for breakfast, but then he was a muesli man through and through. He always had been, it was the most fitting way that he could think of to remember his father. Anyway, it didn't matter, he wasn't there fishing for breakfast, he hoped to catch a memory.

It had been over ten years since he first sat outside that chip shop. In those days he drove a red Fiat Uno and could only dream of cruising the streets in a throbbing machine that bore the name Capri. The Uno was small but it was all Johnny had, and what it lacked in power Johnny made up for in bravado. He wasn't feeling so brave on that first night, however. That fateful evening when he first met Mamma. He had sat there for over an hour, trying to pluck up the courage to go inside. Mamma had a wicked reputation while all Johnny had were the clothes he stood up in (well technically sat down in, he was still in the Uno). He was a tough kid, though, slowly making a name for himself. Sometimes among the right people, mainly amongst the wrong people. At that age he didn't care who they were, as long as they were paying. He would do anything to get out of Greater Londonbury's worst slum, the Burt Reynolds estate, known to locals as

The J.J.'s. So here he was, ready to deal with the devil. An old, Italian female devil.

He stepped out of the car and took a deep breath. He was dressed in dark blue Wranglers with matching denim jacket and Dunlop green flash trainers. He looked the nuts. Johnny ran a hand through his greasy black hair, slicked back and held in place with classic Ray Bans (fake). He took another deep breath; if he didn't move soon he would look like a massive fanny. And in a town where the only currency is pain a fanny finishes last. He found himself wishing for the first time that he smoked and could suck in the sticky, sweet fumes to calm his nerves. He had promised his mother that he would never smoke and so far he hadn't. By the end of this job he would break his mothers heart. Not literally.

A bell above the door jangled as he entered the chip shop. There were no customers, just a tough looking broad behind the counter. Well, she wasn't so much tough looking as she was rough looking. She was a real skank. Johnny noticed her hands were covered in prison tats so he knew not to cross her.

'I'm here about the delivery job,' said Johnny, repeating exactly what he had been told to say. The assistant stared at him blankly and he wondered if she had understood what he had said. He debated whether or not to repeat it, knowing that etiquette was everything to these people. If he spoke out of turn then he could get tortured, killed or worse. Luckily, the fryer made her move and nodded almost imperceptibly towards a door at the back of the shop. 'Thanks,' said Johnny.

The door lead straight onto a steep staircase dimly lit by a single flickering bulb; a 40-watter at the max. Each step that he took produced a painful creak. Johnny cringed every time, not wanting to make a scene. He kept his arms into his body as the walls were peeling and rotten. They almost seemed to pulse with life. After what seemed like an eternity he reached the top. He gathered himself and knocked quickly, the sooner this was over with the better. He couldn't afford to give himself chance to change his mind. A deep voice grunted: 'Come in, you slag.' The slag did as he was told.

Upon entering the room, Johnny reeled as he tried to take in the drastic change in the surroundings. From the squalid exterior, one could never guess the excessive levels of opulence that lay within. This was Mamma Burloni's office and she made sure everyone knew how powerful she was by the sheer extravagance of her fixtures and fittings. Crushed red velvet covered the floor, walls and ceiling. The walls were adorned with expensive looking art, and even Johnny knew that many of them were old masters. Johnny knew that the were supposed to be in some of the world's top art galleries, but he was in no doubt that they were the originals. As if she didn't think that this level of decadence was sufficient, everything else in the room was covered in gold. Even the curtains were made from solid gold, which made them notoriously difficult to draw. In the centre of the room lay a giant desk, which on closer inspection was revealed to be an ornate elephant's head carved entirely from ivory. With some gold bits added on, obviously. It was a very fancy desk, but Johnny wondered how on earth you'd be able to write on it. Stood in the corner of the room was a huge man (although, at a first glance Johnny questioned the creature's humanity) who was the growl that had beckoned Johnny into the room. He would later discover that this was Bertie, Mamma Burloni's fearless bodyguard (and part-time lover). Finally, Johnny looked behind the desk and at its occupant, Mamma herself.

She was as tiny and desiccated as the rumours had suggested. He desperately fought the urge to say, 'Hmm, the force is strong in this one.' He didn't think it would go down too well. She motioned for him to sit. There wasn't a chair. He plonked himself down on the floor. Once he had crossed his legs and looked settled, Mamma began to speak.

'So. You're Johnny Fireheart. I've heard so much about you. You're becoming something of a nuisance. But, don't worry, my boy. I like that. My name, as if you didn't know, is Mamma Burloni, and I have a job offer for you. You can decide not to take it if you wish not too. That is your choice. Of course, if you do turn it down then you would leave me with no choices of my own. Do we understand each other? Good, I thought so. You're a bright boy. On to business. Some of my… associates have become a little sloppy of late. A certain package that I was expecting has been… mislaid. I need this package and I need it now. A woman in my position acquires many… enemies. I would not like to think of the consequences if one of them located it first. I hear you are an expert at locating items that do not wish to be found. Find this for me and I will be very... grateful. Go now. Go to the Club Tropicana and speak to my son, he will tell you all you need to know.'

Johnny stood up and gave a sort of semi-bow; he wasn't really sure what he was supposed to do. He wasn't used to being spoken at for so long. He felt like he should say something, but the gorilla in the corner didn't look like he'd take kindly to it. He moved slowly toward the door not turning his back on Mamma. Johnny had got Mamma confused with the queen, but the additional show of respect wouldn't do any harm. He gingerly reached behind his back and opened the door, moving carefully back onto the landing. As he closed the door he heard the parting words, 'Don't let me down, Johnny.'

The rusty red Fiat squealed as Johnny hit the gas, his body wired with adrenalin. He was relieved to get out of the office in one piece and excited about the prospect of visiting Club Tropicana. It was Greater Londonbury's most exclusive and exotic night spot and prior to this evening Johnny had been neither exclusive nor exotic enough to gain admittance. This time was different. This time he was expected.

He parked in an alley around the corner from the club. As he emerged from the car, he brushed himself down while looking in the wing mirror to check if he was presentable. He concluded that he was presentable enough for The J.J.'s, but nowhere near presentable enough for Club Tropicana. He just had to keep telling himself that he was expected.

Johnny barely noticed the odd doormen, Biff and Quentin, that guarded the club. He was too nervous to care. The bouncers took his nervous nonchalance to be a sign of unbridled confidence, and a decade long uneasy truce was instantly created. They let Johnny pass unchallenged. They'd already been shown his photograph by their boss.

As Johnny entered the club for the first time he instinctively scanned the room. It was dark but he could still recognise many of the faces. The joint was alive with the great and the good of Greater Londonbury. He could make a fortune if he told the press what was going on in there; he just wouldn't be alive long enough to spend it. He looked at the stage and at the beautiful dancers gyrating hypnotically. He could tell by the hungry look in their eyes that they were all hoping to snare a rich boyfriend. He couldn't blame them. Alas, Johnny was beneath their notice so he concentrated on finding Mamma's baby boy. He'd never met Bobby The Lips before but he knew of his reputation. It was almost as gruesome as his mother's. What the hell was Johnny getting himself into. Eventually he spotted a roped off VIP area and made his way toward it. Another Gorilla growled as Johnny approached but the sweaty bald man in the expensive, ill-fitting suit waved him through. This was Burloni. The Lips was entertaining a group of local celebrities, including car dealer Barry Trumpknuts and television weathergirl Sheila Grant. Sat beside Burloni, Johnny gazed upon the most beautiful woman he'd ever laid his eyes on. She was wearing what amounted to sparkly dental floss and her lithe body oozed rampant sexuality. As Johnny approached he couldn't believe his eyes when she smiled at him. It was all he could do to stop his legs turning to jelly and his cock throbbed like a bee sting. He was brought back to earth when he realised that he was being spoken to.

'Sit down my boy,' said Burloni. 'Call me Bobby.'

'Thank you, Mr Burloni, I mean Bobby. Your mother sent me.'

'Yes, yes. There's plenty of time for all of that, my friend. Have some champagne with me and my friends first. Have you met Choo-Choo?' Burloni looked over to goddess who had smiled at Johnny.

'Pleased to meet you, Johnny,' she said, while offering Johnny her hand, which he shook (what did you think he was going to do with it?). Johnny thought that it almost looked as though she was blushing, but surely he was imagining it. Burloni clicked his fingers and a flunky appeared with a fresh bottle of Cristal (it's what all the rappers drink, doncha know). The waiter popped the cork and a small amount frothed over the neck of the bottle

'Dennis Yanney!' exclaimed Burloni. 'Can't you do anything right? You're fired, you knob-cheese. Get the hell out of here!' The waiter slunk away from the VIP area and out of the club forever.

'Calm down, Bobby, it's just a little wine,' soothed Choo-Choo. Johnny wondered if they were lovers. He didn't think he'd be able to stand it if they were. He'd never wanted anybody so much in his life. 'Why don't you go into the back room and discuss your business with Johnny?'

Burloni acquiesced to the beauty's suggestion and motioned for Johnny to follow. They went past yet another heavy into a 'back stage' area occupied by several half naked dancers who squealed and preened as the mobster sleazed his way past them. He patted one or two on the buttocks and they pretended to enjoy it. Being a gangster's moll was like driving down Easy Street. It was literally a piece of cake. The two men finally came to the end of a corridor and stepped into another surprisingly plush office.

Bobby sat down behind the desk and Johnny took the seat opposite. The gangster pushed a fat manila envelope across the desk and Johnny cautiously picked it up. He turned it several times in his hands before he opened it. Inside were a number of black and white photographs. Fireheart felt the bile rise in his throat as he looked upon butchered body after butchered body. He swallowed hard and tried to show no emotion. It was too late to get out. Far too late.

'These photographs were taken in Central America. I can't specify exactly where, for... business reasons. The package my mother wants you to retrieve is somewhere in the jungle. The last team of mercenaries we sent to recover the item are who you see in the photographs. I've heard you're good, Fireheart. Well we're about to see just how damned good you are. You're flying tonight.'

The horror of merely recalling the memory jerked Johnny back into present day. He took a deep breath and made sure that the Capri was still looking good. He mopped his brow as it was slick with sweat. He mopped it in a really cool way though, obviously. It had been years since Johnny had thought about that trip to Central America. Lost in the jungle, being hunted by someone or something, while still trying to find the package. A lot of good men had died on that trip. To be fair, it's quite an interesting story in its own right, but Johnny knew he had to concentrate on the task at hand. Perhaps if I appear in a second novel then I can explore some of my previous adventures, he thought to himself. It didn't matter, the trip to the chippy had done the trick, he knew exactly what he had to do.

Preparations

A few days had passed since that trip to the chippy. Johnny had been a very busy boy and his plans were about to come to fruition. Like an apple. Johnny was glad that this would soon all be over, one way or another. The stress was really taking its toll on him. He'd only been able to sex up Choo-Choo three times in the previous couple of nights and she was starting to become suspicious. He was desperately trying to hide from her that his life was on the line. You could almost say that his life was on the washing line and that Johnny was close to running out of pegs.

Johnny turned the key in the Capri and just listened to the sound of that magnificent engine. It was like a choir of angels after they'd just smoked 40 Woodbines. Beautiful. If he hadn't been Fireheart then he might have shed a tear. But he was Fireheart and so he laughed maniacally instead. He had to be fired up for this journey if he was going to make sure that it wasn't his last. He didn't even say goodbye to Choo-Choo before he left. All women love a bastard. Plus he was too upset to.

As he drove the mean and not-so-mean streets of Greater Londonbury, Johnny knew that this was his place in the world. There wasn't a town that could compare to the old GL and there wasn't a finer man than Johnny Fireheart. He realised that it might sound a little conceited to think such a thing about himself, but you couldn't argue with facts. Johnny knew this first hand, the only fight that he'd ever lost was to a particularly stubborn fact.

As he approached his destination, he took another deep breath and popped a polo mint into his mouth. The mint isn't significant. It's just what happened. His plan was finally being put into action. He just hoped that the secret that sat in the boot of his Capri was going to be his saviour.

Bobby The Lips arrived at Club Tropicana just as Fireheart had asked. There were still a few hours before the nightclub opened and so he knew that there would be ample time to deal with his mother. He'd waited a long time for this moment and he was going to savour it. Like when you have a really nice sausage roll at a buffet.

He walked into the empty club and couldn't see a thing. That's because it was dark. He hadn't gone blind or anything. Let's just say that the lights were off. Because they were.

From out of the gloom stepped Johnny Fireheart. Yes, THE Johnny Fireheart – the one that this whole story has been about. Burloni looked over at him expectantly. Johnny smiled.

'Don't worry, Bobby, I've brought your mother,' said Johnny, and Burloni visibly sighed with relief. 'But, there's one more thing...SURPRISE!!'

At that moment the lights suddenly sprang into action and Bobby could see that the room was actually full of people. He instinctively reached for his gun, but stopped himself when he realised that the place was full of his friends and associates. He was baffled and became only baffleder when he realised that the club had been decorated with balloons, streamers and Happy Birthday banners. It wasn't his freakin' birthday.

The criminal's mind reeled like an old c90 cassette being rewound on a pencil. He was so out of it that he only realised that Johnny and his mother were stood in front of him when they were actually stood in front of him. Before he could react, Johnny took a parcel from Mamma's hand and passed it over to Bobby. You could almost say that they were playing Pass the Parcel, but this was no game. But if it was a game, then you might want to call it that. Regardless of what it was called, Bobby was perplexed.

'Open it,' said Johnny. So he opened it. It was an Atari Lynx games console. He literally couldn't believe his eyes, so much so that he internally called them liars. They were telling the truth, though, it really was an Atari Lynx. It was what he had always wanted.

'I hope you like it, Babba,' said Mamma, with what passed for a smile on her wizened face. Johnny's plan seemed to be working perfectly; he was well chuffed.

The package had been the key to it all along. When Johnny had been sent to retrieve the package from Central America all those years ago, he's assumed that there must have been something illegal involved. After fighting his way through a series of exciting adventures deep within the jungle (which may or may not be documented at a later date), Johnny eventually tracked down the parcel to an abandoned church where it was being guarded by a blind priest. The priest believed that it was an ancient relic that had magical powers, but the young Fireheart couldn't care less for superstition. He took the package like taking toffees from a toddler. Despite himself, he knew that he had to look inside the mysterious package. Curiosity killed the cat, but the dog has bollocks, as the old saying goes. Imagine Johnny's shock when he found that it contained an Atari Lynx games console. He was bamboozled. It's probably a less of a shock to you folks because it's already been mentioned, but just put yourselves in Johnny's shoes for a minute...I'll wait while you do it.

There.

Shocking, wasn't it?

He flew the precious cargo back to Greater Londonbury immediately and delivered it straight into Mamma Burloni's hands. He's never seen a prune looking ecstatic, but he imagined that it would look a lot like Mamma. She ripped the parcel open immediately and began to inspect the video game housed within. The look on her face changed in an instant. The console was riddled with bullet holes.

'Noooooooooo,' screamed Mamma. 'Whatsa my boy gonna do for his a birthday? This is a the last one in da country!' It was a well known fact that Mamma turned stereotypically Italian when she was proper livid and Johnny knew that he had to be like a railway engineer and make tracks. He didn't want to be on the end of a verbal tongue-lashing. Or worse. He knew that something bad was going to come from this weird, retro-console related incident and so he blanked it from his mind for a full ten years. Until just a few days ago.

Johnny had realised that Bobby's feud with his own mother was nothing more than a spoilt child lashing out for not getting the present that he really wanted. It was quite pathetic really and hardly seemed to justify an 8000 word story. Luckily for Johnny, he was able to find a replacement console on a popular internet auction site. Yes, you know the one I'm talking about. Johnny even found one available that was 'pick up only' and so he didn't even have to wait for it to be posted. All he had to to then was to arrange a surprise birthday party for Bobby. It wasn't easy at such short notice, but Johnny was a dab hand at whipping up a buffet.

Fireheart looked at Mamma and Bobby and was overjoyed to see them embrace, even though it turned his stomach. To be fair, they were both hideous. That didn't matter now. All that mattered was that Johnny Fireheart lived to fight another day.

What a guy.

THE END

1604523R0

Printed in Great Britain
by Amazon.co.uk, Ltd.,
Marston Gate.